More Chicken Soup

·AND· ·OTHER· ·FOLK· ·REMEDIES·

JOAN WILEN AND LYDIA WILEN

ILLUSTRATIONS BY
ELIZABETH KODA-CALLAN

Fawcett Columbine • New York

A Fawcett Columbine Book
Published by Ballantine Books
Copyright © 1986 by Joan Wilen and Lydia Wilen
Illustrations copyright © 1984, 1986 by Elizabeth Koda-Callan
All rights reserved under International and Pan-American
Copyright Conventions. Published in the United States
by Ballantine Books,
a division of Random House, Inc.,
New York, and simultaneously in
Canada by Random House of Canada Limited, Toronto.

Grateful acknowledgment is made to the Mayo Clinic for
permission to reprint an excerpt from *The Mayo Clinic Health Letter*
entitled "Reliable Information for a Healthier Life," October
1964, Vol. 2, no. 10. Reprinted by permission of The Mayo
Clinic, Rochester, MN 55905.

Library of Congress Catalog Card Number: 86:90737

ISBN: 0-449-90192-0

Text design by Beth Tondreau
Cover illustration by Elizabeth Koda-Callan

Manufactured in the United States of America

First Edition: November 1986
10 9 8 7

MORE CHICKEN SOUP AND OTHER FOLK REMEDIES
is dedicated to people who are
dedicated to helping heal others.

Contents

REMEDIES

Acknowledgments

A BIG THANK YOU to friends and family who offered us their loving support, good wishes and remedies.

SPECIAL THANKS to:

Eileen Nock
Heather Brodhead
Judy Twersky
Arlen Hollis Kane
Michael L. Samuels
Barbara Carpenter
Martha Neag and Marie Neag
Paul Schulick
Ruth Lesser
Andy Port
Ted Brown
Ronald E. Franzmeier
Ruth Landa
Priscilla Serafin
Robert Pardi
Nick Malekos
Janine Pietrucha
J. Walter Allen
Barbara Landgarten-Schulick
Gotham Group of Hadassah
Cynthia Bernbach-Pearlman
Dick Syatt
Patricia Burke
Dorothy Senerchia
Allen Tobias
George Nider
Blanche Miller
Otto Pietrucha
Linda Guss
Jane Biberman
Owen Spann
Tom Bergeron
Myles P. Burton
Richard A. Perozzi

And all the TV shows, radio shows, newspapers and magazines that have helped us get the word out on *CHICKEN SOUP & OTHER FOLK REMEDIES.*

Our gratitude to Leona Nevler for helping us start it all with our first folk remedy book; to John Molish for championing our cause; and, our appreciation to all the people who bought copies of it, making this sequel possible.

Our thanks to Andrea Laine whose enthusiasm and help mean a lot to us.

EXTRA SPECIAL THANKS to Joelle Delbourgo for being the driving force behind *MORE CHICKEN SOUP*.

And we thank our lucky stars for our editor, Michelle Russell.

Introduction

When we were growing up in Brooklyn, each winter my mom would crochet little drawstring bags and my dad would see to it they were filled with camphor, which he then insisted we wear around our necks. Daddy was sure that it would prevent us from catching colds. We reeked so from the camphor, none of our friends would come near us, and we didn't catch their colds. Daddy was right.

When we'd walk into a room, the camphor smell was so strong that we'd joke, "We weren't born, we were just taken out of storage."

That camphor was our introduction to folk remedies . . . along with honey and lemon for a sore throat, sugar water for the hiccups, horseradish to clear the sinuses, garlic for a whole bunch of things, and chicken soup for everything else.

Our mom made the world's best chicken soup . . . when she wasn't crocheting little drawstring bags for the camphor. In fact, the soup recipe is in our first book, *Chicken Soup & Other Folk Remedies*.

With the exception of a few important remedies we would have been remiss in not repeating (including chicken soup for a cold), this book is a whole new collection of remedies from sources all over the world. Many people saw us on TV, heard us on radio, or read

xiv • INTRODUCTION

our first book, and were kind enough to share their own
folk remedies with us.

In our first book, we limited ourselves to ingredients
everyone knows and probably has in their kitchens. In
this book, we're a little more daring in terms of fruits,
vegetables, vitamins, minerals and herbs. We feel sure
that all of you are ready to expand your range of choices
and to grow with the times. Why else would these fruits,
vegetables, vitamins, minerals and herbs be readily
available at supermarkets, greengrocers, health food stores
and herb farms throughout the country? (Please check
the back of the book for a list of reliable suppliers.)

Since lots of the remedies called for ingredients and
procedures that were new to us, we did a tremendous
amount of experimenting. Oh yes, we shopped around
for herbs, made poultices, sprouted seeds, drank all
kinds of concoctions, cooked, baked, boiled, roasted,
steamed, soaked, scrubbed, grated, minced, diced,
spiced, blended, whipped, whisked, powdered, peeled
and did extensive research and testing of dosages.

It was quite an education for both of us. We can fill
another book with our experiences. Once, while experimenting with bee pollen dosages, we knew that
Joan had taken too much. She had this uncontrollable
urge to fling herself against a screen door.

But seriously . . .

To insure your safety, a medical doctor has reviewed
every remedy in the book and, while he still may be
scratching his head at the effectiveness of some of the
more unconventional remedies, he concluded that they
may not always help, but they certainly wouldn't hurt.

Please, for your own well being, be sure to consult
with a health professional before starting any self-help
health treatment.

Our home remedy suggestions are, for the most part, scientifically unproven and should not take the place of professional health care that may be needed for certain ailments and for persistent symptoms.

We have no formal medical training and are not prescribing treatment, merely reporting folk remedies.

Incidentally, since you seem to be interested in folk remedies, we would love your input. Have you tried any of these remedies? What has been your experience with them?

Do you have any of your own remedies you would like to share with us?

We can be reached by mail at the address below.

Thank you for reading our book.

To your health,

Joan Wilen

Lydia Wilen

Joan Wilen and Lydia Wilen
P.O. Box 416
Ansonia Station
New York, NY 10023

More
Chicken
Soup

·AND· ·OTHER· ·FOLK· ·REMEDIES·

Preparation Guide

Throughout this book, you will find remedies requiring a bit of preparation. Here we tell you how.

‡ POULTICES

Poultices are usually made with vegetables, fruit or herbs that are either minced, chopped, grated, crushed, mashed and sometimes cooked. These ingredients are then wrapped in a clean fabric—cheesecloth, white cotton, unbleached muslin—and applied externally to the affected area.

A poultice is said to be effective when moist. After a few hours, when the poultice dries out, it should be changed—the cloth as well as the ingredients.

Whenever possible, use fresh fruits, vegetables or herbs. If these are unavailable, then use dried herbs. To soften the herb, pour hot water over it. Do not let it steep in boiling water. The herb can lose its effectiveness, particularly in the case of comfrey.

Let's use comfrey as an example of a typical poultice. Cut a piece of cloth twice the size of the area it will cover. If you're using a fresh leaf, wash it with cool water, then crush it in your hand. Place the leaf on one half of the cloth and fold over the other half. If you are making a poultice with dried comfrey root and leaves, pour hot water over the herb, then place the softened herb on half of the cloth, fold over the other half and apply it to the affected body part. Put an Ace bandage or another strip of cloth around the poultice to hold it in place.

‡ POMANDERS

To make an orange-spice pomander, you'll need:

1 thin-skinned orange
1 box of whole cloves
1 ounce orrisroot
1 ounce cinnamon
½ ounce nutmeg
2 feet ¼"–½" ribbon

Tie the ribbon around the orange. Stick the cloves all over the orange, except for where the ribbon is. Place it in a bowl with the three herbs and let it stay there for 4 to 5 days, turning it occasionally. Then hang the pomander in a closet.

‡ BARLEY WATER

Boil 2 ounces of barley in 6 cups of water until there's about half the water—3 cups—left in the pot. Strain. If necessary, add honey and lemon to taste.

‡ GENERAL RECIPE FOR HERB TEAS

Place a teaspoonful of the herb, or a tea bag, in a glass or ceramic cup and pour just-boiled water over it. (The average water-to-herb ratio is 1 cup of water to 1 teaspoonful of herb.) Let the herb steep for 5 to 10 minutes, then strain. If you must have it sweetened, then add some raw honey. (Never add sugar because it negates the value of most herbs.) Drink slowly.

‡ SPROUTING ALFALFA SEEDS

You're going to need alfalfa seeds, a 1-gallon jar, a rubber band for the neck of the jar, nylon mesh or cheesecloth and a dish rack or some kind of stand.

Fill the jar halfway with lukewarm water, preferably filtered. Soak 3 tablespoonsful of alfalfa seeds in the jar overnight (anywhere from 5 to 8 hours).

Put the mesh or cheesecloth over the mouth of the jar, securing it with the rubber band. After the soaking, pour out the water. Turn the jar upside down and at a 45-degree angle, resting it on the dish rack or stand, making sure the jar's opening allows air in and is not completely covered up by seeds. Let it stand in a dark area. Twice a day (about every 12 hours), fill the jar with cool water, giving the seeds a good rinse, then pour out the water and continue letting it drain in the dark until the next rinse cycle.

When the sprouts are about 1¼ inches long (after 4 or 5 days), put them in the sun or under a grow-light for a day and watch them turn green as they manufacture chlorophyll.

To harvest the sprouts, place them in a bowl, basin or sink filled with water. The hulls will rise to the surface. Scoop off the hulls and put the hull-less sprouts back in the jar, turned upside down to allow the excess water to drain off. Once drained, they're ready to be eaten and/or refrigerated. They will keep fresh several days.

One pound of seed makes approximately 8 pounds of sprouts.

Sprouting is a lot less complicated than the instructions sound. Once you get into it, you might want to try sprouting mung beans, lentils, radish seeds, aduki beans and fenugreek seeds.

According to some medical experts and nutritional researchers, sprouts come as close to being the "perfect food" as anything available.

‡ SPROUTING CHART

A 1-gallon jar for the seeds will allow them lots of room to sprout. Delicatessens have gallon pickle jars and health food restaurants have gallon fruit cocktail jars they're usually willing to give away.

‡ DRY-ROASTING SUNFLOWER SEEDS

Place a handful of shelled, unprocessed sunflower seeds in a pan, over low heat. Stay with them for the 2-or-so minutes it takes for them to roast. Jiggle them along the way so that both sides get done. When you hear them crackle and see several of them move by themselves, they're ready.

Dry-roasting makes the seeds remarkably flavorful.

Seeds	Amount	Soak Time (Hours)	When Ready (Days)	Harvest Length (Inches)	Notes
Alfalfa	3–4 Tbs.	5–8	4–5	1–1½	Place in sun 8–10 hours to develop chlorophyll before harvesting.
Fenugreek	1 cup	6–8	3–4	⅓–¾	Use sparingly.
Radish	½ cup	4–6	4–5	1–½	Place in sun 8–10 hours to develop chlorophyll before harvesting. Strong tasting; mix with other sprouts.
Lentils	1 cup	12	2–3	¼–¾	Eat them short or long.
Aduki	1 cup	12	3–5	¼–¾	Allow for a lot of soak water.
Mung	1 cup	12	4–5	1–2	For each rinsing, allow mung beans to stay in cold water for one minute.

‡ AN HERBAL BATH

To prepare an herbal bath, simply take a handful of one or a combination of your favorite dried or fresh herbs, and place them in the center of a white handkerchief. Secure the herbs in the handkerchief by turning it into a little knapsack. Toss the herb-filled knapsack into the tub and let the water run. Then enjoy your bath.

After your bath, open the handkerchief and spread the herbs out to dry. You can use them again 2 or 3 times.

For starters, you may want to try a combination called, "Loving Bath Herbs"—it's sandalwood, orrisroot, and myrrh. According to *An Ancient Book of Formulas*, this is said to have a calming effect on the people with whom the bather meets, after the bath, of course.

Remedies

‡Arthritis (Rheumatism, Bursitis, Gout)

There are many forms of arthritis and rheumatism. And there are many folk remedies that may help heal those conditions, or at least offer relief from those painful conditions.

You can try more than one remedy at a time. For instance, drink white grape juice in the morning; have sage tea later in the day; give yourself a ginger/sesame oil rub at night. While you're trying these remedies, pay attention to your body and you'll soon learn what makes you feel better.

White grape juice is said to absorb the system's acid. Drink 1 glassful in the morning and 1 glassful before dinner.

If you have morning stiffness caused by arthritis, try sleeping in a sleeping bag. You can sleep *on* your bed, but *in* the zipped up bag. It's much more effective than an electric blanket because your body heat is evenly distributed and retained. Come morning, there's less pain, making it easier to get going.

Corn silk tea has been known to reduce acid in the system and lessen pain. Steep a handful of the silky strings that grow around ears of corn in a cup of hot water for 10 minutes. If it's not fresh-corn season, buy corn silk extract in a health food store and add 10 to 15 drops in 1 cup of water and drink. Dried corn silk can also be used. Prepare it as you would prepare an herbal tea. You can get dried corn silk at most places that sell dried herbs (see "Sources").

Each of these herbs are known as pain reducers: sage, rosemary, nettles and basil. Also, add alfalfa seeds to the list. Use any one, two, three, four or five of them in the form of tea (see "Preparation Guide"). Have a couple of cups a day, rotating them until you find which makes you feel best.

My friend's grandfather cleared up an arthritic condition and lived to be 90, following a remedy given to him by a woman who brought it here from Puerto Rico. Squeeze the juice of a large lime into a cup of black coffee and drink it hot first thing each morning. We're not in favor of drinking coffee, but who are we to argue with success?

An old American Indian arthritis remedy is a mixture of mashed yucca root and water. PLEASE KEEP READING! Yucca saponin, a steroid derivative of the yucca plant, is a forerunner of cortisone. The side effects of cortisone are too numerous and unpleasant to mention. The side effects of yucca, according to a double-blind study done at a Southern California arthritis clinic, were relief from headaches as well as gastrointestinal complaints. Sixty percent of the patients taking yucca tablets for that study showed dramatic improvements in their arthritic conditions. It tells us that while it doesn't work for everyone, it works for a large enough number of people to make it worth a try.

For most people, this remedy is not practical; for many, it's not even possible. Then why take up all this space? The results reported to us were so spectacular, that we feel if only one person reads this, follows through and is relieved of their painful, debilitating condition, it will have been well worth the space on the page.

When we were given this Mexican remedy, we were told that it's for all kinds of "rheumatic" conditions. Some health professionals believe "arthritis" and "rheumatism" are the same, although we could not find a definitive answer. If you're considering trying this remedy, we leave it up to you and your medical consultant to discern whether or not yours is a "rheumatic" condition.

Starting with the first set of directions, you will see why this is usually a "last resort" remedy.

Bring a couple of truckloads of ocean sand to your yard. (What did we tell you?) Select a sheltered spot away from the wind. Dig a hole about 12 feet by 12 feet and about 3 feet deep, then dump the sand in it.

You will, obviously, need help in setting up the above. You will also need help to carry out the treatment. Incidentally, treatment should take place on hot summer days.

Wear a brief bathing suit, lie on your stomach with your face to the side (so you can breathe, of course), and have your body completely covered with sand, except for your head. Stay that way for 15 minutes. Next, turn over on your back and have your body completely covered with sand, except for your head and face. Have your assistant put sunscreen on your face. Stay that way for 15 minutes. Then get out of the sandbath, quickly cover yourself with a warm flannel or woolen robe and head for the shower. Take a hot shower, dry off thoroughly and go to bed for several hours (3 to 4) and relax. During all of this, make sure there's no exposure to the wind or to any drafts.

According to an Oriental saying: "Rheumatism goes out from the body only through sweating."

During the next couple of hours in bed, you may have to change underwear several times because of profuse sweating. This is good.

One sandbath a day is sufficient. For some people, one week of treatments has been enough to help heal the condition completely.

NOTE: The sandbath must have dry sand, be in your yard, in an area that's sheltered from the wind. The beach is too wet, too breezy and usually too far from home.

Drink ⅛ teaspoon of cayenne pepper in a glass of water or fruit juice (cherry juice without sugar or preservatives is best). If the pepper is just too strong for you, buy #1 capsules and fill them with cayenne, or you can buy already-prepared cayenne capsules at the health food store. Take 2 a day.

Combine ½ teaspoonful of eucalyptus oil, available at health food stores, with 1 tablespoonful of pure olive oil, and massage the mixture into your painful areas.

You may want to alternate the above massage mixture with this one: grate fresh ginger, then squeeze the juice through a piece of cheesecloth. Mix the ginger juice with an equal amount of sesame oil. Massage it on the painful areas. Ginger can be quite strong. If you are uncomfortable from the burning sensation, tone down the ginger by adding more sesame oil to the mixture.

Aloe vera gel is now being used for lots of ailments, including arthritis. You can apply the gel externally to the aching joint and you can take it internally—1 tablespoonful in the morning before breakfast and 1 tablespoonful before dinner.

Vegetable juices are wonderful for everyone. They can be particularly helpful for arthritis sufferers. Use *fresh* carrot juice as a sweetener with either celery juice or kale juice. (Invest in a juicer or connect with a nearby juice bar.)

‡ GOUT

Isn't it amazing how much pain you can have from one toe? If you have gout, you probably know it's time to change your diet. The closer you stick to vegetarian cuisine, the faster the gout will go. Okay, eat some fish and lean chicken now and then, but stay away from meat for a while. Also eliminate sugar and white flour from your diet. You may start feeling so good, you may never want to go back to those things.

The one remedy everyone seems to agree on: cherries. Eat them fresh or frozen. Also, drink pure cherry juice daily.

Soak your goutful foot in comfrey tea (see "Preparation Guide").

A Russian remedy is raw garlic—2 cloves a day. The best way to take raw garlic cloves is to mince them, put them in water (better yet, in cherry juice) and drink them down. No chewing necessary. Your garlic breath will disappear within an hour. It doesn't linger on your breath, but it may repeat on you. So does a salami sandwich and this is a helluva lot healthier.

✣Asthma

Our hearts go out to you asthma sufferers. We've worked especially hard to find effective remedies for this especially troublesome ailment.

We haven't found a sure cure, but we have heard about some remedies that work for some people. While looking for the one that can control your condition, please consult with your health professional every step of the way.

We heard about a man who was able to ease off massive doses of cortisone by using garlic therapy. He started with 1 clove a day, minced, in a couple of ounces of orange juice. He gulped it down without chewing any of the little pieces of garlic. That way, he didn't have garlic on his breath for any length of time. As he increased the number of garlic cloves he ate each day, his doctor decreased the amount of cortisone he was taking. After several months, he was eating 6 to 10 cloves of garlic a day, he was completely off cortisone, and was not bothered by asthma.

At the first sign of asthma-type wheezing, saturate 2 strips of white cloth in white vinegar and wrap them around your wrists, not too tightly. For some people, it stops a full-blown attack from developing.

Generally, dairy products are not good for asthmatics. They're too mucus-forming. We have heard, though, that cheddar cheese might be an exception. It contains "tyramine," an ingredient that seems to help open up the breathing passages.

As strange as this sounds, we've gotten this remedy from several sources. A muskrat skin worn over the lungs with the fur side to the body is supposed to give relief to asthma sufferers. Your local furrier should be able to get a muskrat skin for you. Make sure it's a "natural" skin—no brightener or dye added. It should be golden, orangy brown with yellowish-beige leather. One skin should cost anywhere from $8 to $15.

Cut a 1-ounce stick of licorice (the kind with the bark on it, not the candy kind) into slices and steep the slices in a quart of just-boiled water for 24 hours. Strain and bottle. At the first sign of a heaviness on the chest, drink a cup of the licorice water. A word of caution, however: licorice may cause fluid retention and should be used in moderation for people with kidney conditions or high blood pressure.

NOTE (or should we say, WARNING?): In France, licorice water is a drink used by women to give them more sexual vitality.

We were on a radio show when a woman called in and shared her asthma remedy: cherry bark tea. She buys tea bags in a health food store (if teas are alphabetically listed, it may be under "w" for "wild cherry bark tea"), and she drinks a cup before each meal and another cup at bedtime. The woman swore to us that it has changed her life. She hasn't had an asthma attack since she's started taking it five years ago.

This remedy requires a juicer or a nearby juice bar. Drink equal amounts of endive (also called chicory), celery and carrot juice. A glassful of the juice a day works wonders for some asthmatics.

Roast 3 eggshells for 2 hours at 400 degrees. The shells will turn light brown. (They'll also smell like rotten eggs.) Smash them into little bits and mix them into a cup of unsulphured molasses. Take 1 teaspoonful before each meal. It just may prevent an asthma condition from acting up.

For this first-aid remedy, you'll need a sugar cube and eucalyptus oil (see "Sources"). When you have a heaviness on your chest that makes breathing difficult, put 1 drop of the oil on 1 sugar cube and let it melt in your mouth.

‡Back

In our first folk remedy book, we didn't touch on back problems at all, figuring there are almost as many good books on bad backs as there are bad backs. And there are bad backs! It is estimated that 8 out of 10 people have, at some point in their lives, back pain that disables them. Also estimated is the money spent each year for diagnosis and treatment of back pain—over $5 billion.

Since writing that first book, we've come across some back remedies worth reporting. At best, they'll help; at least, they'll give you something to talk about next time someone tells you their back went out.

We are antismoking, to the point where Lydia belongs to an organization that lobbies for nonsmokers' rights. We were happy to find one more reason *not* to smoke—a condition called "smoker's back." According to a study done at the University of Vermont, back pains are more common and more frequent among smokers. They theorize that it has to do with the effect of nicotine on the carbon monoxide levels in the blood, which causes the smoker to cough and the cough, in turn, puts a tremendous strain on the back. Yup! One more good reason to STOP SMOKING! (For suggestions on how to quit, see: "Smoke Stoppers.")

You need to employ the buddy system for this remedy. Get your buddy to put 20 drops of eucalyptus oil in a tablespoon and warm it by putting a lit match under the spoon for a few seconds. Then have that buddy gently massage the warm oil on your painful area. The "hands on" are as healing as the oil.

Thanks to the guidance of our cousin, Linda, who is a physical therapist, many people who have felt that their backs were on the verge of going out, didn't. If you have had back trouble, you know the feeling we're referring to. Carefully lie down on the floor, close enough to a sofa or easy chair so that you can bend your knees and rest your legs (knees to feet) on the seat of the sofa or chair. Your thighs should be leaning against the front of the sofa and your tush should be as close as possible, directly in front of it, with the rest of your body flat on the floor. (Carpeting is a bonus.) In that position, you're like the start of a staircase. Your body is the lowest step, your thighs are the distance between the steps and your knees-to-feet are the second step. (Did I just confuse you instead of painting a clear picture? Once you're on the floor, it's easy to figure out.)

I stay in that position from 15 to 30 minutes and find it's a restful and healing treatment for my back.

The best and safest way to get up is to roll over on your side, then slowly lift yourself up, letting your arms and shoulders do most of the work.

FOR MEN ONLY: Do you have back or hip pains when you sit for any length of time? Is it something you and your doctor(s) can't quite figure out and so you label it "back trouble"? According to Dr. Elmar Lutz of St. Mary's Hospital in New Jersey, you may need a "walletectomy." If you carry around a thick, bursting-at-the-seams wallet in your hip pocket, it may be causing pressure on the sciatic nerve. How do you spell relief? J-a-c-k-e-t p-o-c-k-e-t! Keep your wallet in your jacket pocket and you'll find sitting can be a pleasurable experience.

The rocking chair was invented here in the United States. In England, it became known as the "American common-sense chair." Dr. Barry Wyke of the Royal College of Surgeons in London is one of the world's foremost authorities on back problems. Through studies conducted at Royal College, Dr. Wyke concluded that rocking chairs can help a royal pain. The rocking motion seems to block nerve impulses that produce lower back pain. Rocking is good for circulation and also has a relaxing effect, which is important in our generally tension-laden lives. So as not to disappoint our audience, we feel obliged to end with: So, don't go off your rocker!

At one time it was hard for most people to believe that what we eat affects our state of health. Now that most of us understand that it's so, we can talk about food and lower back problems.

Eating white sugar and drinking sugary drinks is the worst thing you could do for your lower back. The body's process of metabolizing sugar taxes the adrenal glands, spleen, pancreas and kidneys and puts an added strain on the lower back. For many health reasons, including protection of the lower back, stay away from food and drinks containing sugar.

Limit your intake of liquids, especially alcoholic beverages. If you drink lots of liquids, you overwork the kidneys and weaken the lower back. The ideal way of life is to eat foods with a high water content (steamed vegetables, raw salads and fruit), and then you don't need to supplement your diet with many additional liquids.

An Oriental remedy for the prevention or relief of lower back problems is black beans, available at supermarkets and health food stores.

Soak a cupful of the black beans (also called frijoles negros), overnight. This softens the beans and is said to remove the gas-producing compounds. Then, put them in a pot with 3½ cups of water. Bring to a boil, then let simmer for ½ hour over low heat. During that ½ hour, keep removing the grayish foam that forms on top. After ½ hour, cover the pot and let it cook for another 2 hours. If by the end of that time, there's still water in the pot, spill it out.

Eat 2 to 3 tablespoonsful of the black beans a day, every day for 1 month; then every other day for 1 month.

Fresh beans should be prepared at least every 3 or 4 days.

If you need to salt the beans, use a little "tamari"—natural soy sauce available at supermarkets and health food stores.

At the end of 2 months, if you no longer have lower back pain and you attribute it to the black beans, continue eating them every other day. If you feel your back problem would have healed anyway, stop eating the beans. And, at the first sign of pain in the lower back area, go back to the beans.

Try a flaxseed poultice for chronic back pain (see "Preparation Guide"). Soak 1 cup of flaxseeds in cold water for 10 hours. In an enamel or glass saucepan, bring the flaxseeds to a boil. As soon as it's cool enough to the hand, but still as hot as can be without scalding yourself, make a poultice of the seeds and place it on the painful area. You can keep reheating the flaxseeds and reapplying new poultices.
CAUTION: DO NOT APPLY HEAT TO ACUTE BACK PAIN, ONLY TO CHRONIC PAIN. IF YOU HAVE ANY QUESTION ABOUT WHETHER YOU HAVE CHRONIC OR ACUTE BACK PAIN, DON'T USE HEAT!

We know a chiropractor who specializes in helping dancers and athletes. He prescribes vitamin C—500 mg after each meal—to ease the pain and speed the healing of lower back conditions.

Have you ever had an ice rubdown? The thought of it sends chills up my spine, but it may help relieve the pain in that very same area. An easy way to do it is by freezing a polystyrene cupful of water. Then, peel off about ½-inch of the cup's lip and use the rest of the cup as a sort of knob or handle, gliding the iced surface over your back. One thing you don't want to do is strain yourself trying to reach your painful parts, so you may want to ask a friend to give you the rubdown. Say, you might want to ask a friend to give you the rubdown even if you don't have back pain.

‡Blood Pressure

When blood pressure is measured, there are two numbers reported: the first and higher number is the systolic. It measures the pressure inside the arteries the second the heart beats. The diastolic is the lower number and measures the pressure in the arteries when the heart is at rest.

We saw a woman wearing a T-shirt that said: "Anybody with normal blood pressure these days, just isn't paying attention."

More than 20 million Americans have high blood pressure (hypertension). If you're one of those people, obviously you're not alone.

We urge you to take a look at your lifestyle and, once and for all, do something to change whatever is causing the blood pressure problem.

You probably already know the following basics, but in case you need to review them:

- If you're overweight, diet sensibly (without diet pills). Eliminate salt (use sea salt in moderation), and cut down or cut out red meat.
- To reduce the stress of your everyday life, try meditation, or some self-help program. Ask a health professional for guidance and reputable contacts.
- If you smoke, stop! (See "Smoke Stoppers.")
- If you drink, stop! Or at least cut down drastically.

Read on for additional high and low blood pressure health hints.

‡ HIGH BLOOD PRESSURE

Cayenne (red) pepper is a wonderful blood pressure stabilizer. Add ⅛ teaspoonful to a cup of goldenseal tea (see "Sources") and drink a cupful daily.

In a blender, or with a mortar and pestle, crush 2 teaspoonsful of dried watermelon seeds. Put them in a cup of just-boiled water and let them steep for 1 hour. Stir, strain and drink that cupful of watermelon seed tea ½ hour before a meal. Repeat the procedure before each meal, 3 times a day. After taking the tea for a few days, have your pressure checked and see if it works for you, or if this watermelon remedy is the pits.

Incidentally, watermelon seeds are known to tone up kidney function. Be prepared to use bathroom facilities often. Also, watermelon-seed tea can be bought at health food stores.

How would you like a hot or cold cup of raspberry leaf tea? It may help bring down your blood pressure. Combine 1 ounce of raspberry leaves to 2 cups of boiling water and simmer for 20 minutes in an enamel or glass saucepan. Drink 1 cup a day, hot or cold (no ice cubes), and in a week, check the results by having your blood pressure taken.

The faster you talk, the less oxygen you have coming in. The less oxygen, the harder the blood has to work to maintain the supply of oxygen. The harder the blood has to work, the higher the blood pressure seems to go. If that makes sense, please explain it to us. The bottom line here is that if you talk slower, theoretically you will take bigger and better breaths, giving you more oxygen and preventing your blood pressure from climbing, sort of.

We've promised our readers, our editor and ourselves that we wouldn't repeat remedies that were in our first folk remedy book. A promise is a promise, and so we will not talk about garlic, apples or fish tanks. We will ask that you do yourselves (and us and our publisher) a favor and get a copy of our first *Chicken Soup* book, so you can also look into those other effective blood pressure remedies. Thank you!

‡ LOW BLOOD PRESSURE

We heard from a Russian folk healer who recommends drinking ½ cup of raw beet juice when a person feels that his or her blood pressure may be a little too low. This healer also told us that a person with low blood pressure *knows* that feeling.

Deep breathing may bring blood pressure levels up to normal. First thing in the morning and last thing at night, do this breathing exercise: let all the air out of your lungs—exhale, squeezing all the old air out—then let the air in through your nostrils, slowly to the count of 7. When no more air will fit in your lungs, hold tight for the count of 14. Next, gently let the air out through your mouth to the count of 7—all the way out. Inhale and exhale this way 10 times, twice a day.

Even when your blood pressure is normal, continue this breathing exercise for all kinds of physical benefits.

‡Body Odour
**(We think the British spelling
makes it seem less gross.)**

If you have a problem with bad-smelling armpits, raise your hand. Oops!—better not. Instead, take a shower, then prepare turnip juice. Grate a turnip, squeeze the juice through cheesecloth so that you have 2 teaspoonsful. *Now* raise your hand and vigorously massage a teaspoonful of the turnip juice into each armpit.

A vegetarian friend's sense of smell is so keen, she can stand next to someone and tell whether (s)he is a meat eater. If you are a heavy meat eater and are troubled by body odour, change your diet. Ease off meat and force yourself to fill up on green leafy vegetables. There will be a big difference in a short time. You probably won't perspire less, but the smell won't be as strong. That change of diet will be healthier for you in general. And it will be appreciated by all the people in all the crowded elevators you will ever get on.

In addition to eating green leafy vegetables, take a 500 mg capsule of wheat grass (powdered juice) daily. Be sure to take it on an empty stomach and drink it down with spring water. The chlorophyll can decrease body odour dramatically.

If tension causes you to perspire excessively, which then causes unpleasant body odours, drink sage tea. Use 1½ teaspoonsful of dried sage, or 2 tea bags in 1 cup of water. Let it steep for 10 minutes. Drink it in small doses throughout the day.

‡Burns

When gathering material for the "Burns" section of our first folk remedy book, we called several burn centers throughout the country to make sure we had our facts straight. Although, for the most part, we have not repeated remedies, we feel obligated to repeat this important first aid information from our other book.

Burns are classified by degrees. A first-degree burn involves painful, red, unbroken skin. A second-degree burn involves painful blisters and broken skin. A third-degree burn destroys underlying tissue as well as surface skin. It may be painless because nerve endings may have also been destroyed. A fourth-degree burn involves deeply charred and blackened areas of the skin.

Second-degree burns that cover an extensive area of skin and all third- and fourth-degree burns require immediate medical attention. Any kind of burn on the face should also receive immediate medical attention as a precaution against swollen breathing passages.

For first-degree burns—grabbing a hot pot handle, grasping the iron side of an iron, the oven door closing on your forearm, a splattering of boiling oil—here are first-aid suggestions using mostly handy household items.

‡ FIRST-DEGREE BURNS

Apply cold water or cold compresses first! Then—

Draw out the heat and pain by applying a slice of raw, unpeeled potato, or a piece of fresh pumpkin pulp, or a slice of raw onion. Leave the potato, pumpkin or onion on the burn for 15 minutes, off for 5 minutes and put a fresh piece on for another 15 minutes.

If you burn yourself when there's an uncooked chicken around, place the chicken fat directly on the burn or scald. It's said to be extremely soothing.

Puncture either a vitamin E or garlic oil capsule and squeeze the contents directly on the burn.

If you have a smooth piece of charcoal, put it on the burn and keep it there for an hour. Within minutes, the pain may begin to subside.

If you're outdoors, pack mud on the burn to draw out the heat.

People have had remarkable results with apple cider vinegar. Pour it on the burned or scalded area.

Keep an aloe vera plant in your home. It's like growing a tube of ointment. Break off about a ½-inch piece of stem. Squeeze it so that the juice oozes out onto the burned area. The juice is most effective if the plant is as least 2 to 3 years old and the stems have little bumps on the edges.

‡ SECOND-DEGREE BURNS

For at *least* ½ hour, dip the burned area in cold water. DO NOT USE LARD, BUTTER OR A SALVE ON THE BURN! Those things seal in the heat and when you get medical attention, the doctor has to wipe off the goo to see the condition of the skin.

If the burn is on an arm or leg, keep the limb raised in the air to help prevent swelling.

‡ CHEMICAL AND ACID BURNS

Until you get medical attention, immediately get the affected area under the closest running water—a sink, a garden hose or the shower. The running water will help wash the chemicals off the skin. Keep the water running on the burned skin for at least 20 minutes or until medical help arrives.

‡ BURNED TONGUE

Keep rinsing your mouth with cold water. A few drops of vanilla extract on the tongue may relieve the pain.

Ease the pain of a burned tongue by sprinkling some white sugar on it.

‡ ROPE BURNS

Soak the hands in salt water. If salt and water are not available, do as they do in Italy for rope burns: soak the hands in urine.

‡ SUNBURN

When you've gotten more than you've basked for, fill a quart jar with equal parts of milk and ice and 2 tablespoonsful of salt. Soak a washcloth in the mixture and place it on the sunburned area. Leave it on for about 15 minutes. Repeat the procedure 3 to 4 times throughout the day.

Make a healing lotion by beating the white of an egg and mixing in 1 teaspoonful of castor oil. Gently rub it on the sunburned skin.

Or, you may want to empty a package of powdered nonfat dry milk or a quart of regular low-fat milk into a tub of warm water, and spend the next half hour soaking in it, soothing your sunburn.

NOTE: Severe sunburns can be second-degree burns. If the skin is broken or blistering, treatment should include cold water followed by a dry (preferably sterile) dressing.

‡ SUNBURN PAIN PREVENTION
One way to prevent a sunburn from hurting is by taking a hot, yes hot, shower right after sunbathing. According to a homeopathic principle, the hot water desensitizes the skin.

‡ SUNBURN PREVENTION
Mix an equal amount of olive oil with apple cider vinegar. Shake vigorously and apply it to the areas of your body that will be exposed to the sun.

‡ SUNBURNED EYES AND EYELIDS

Make a poultice of grated apples and rest it on your closed eyelids for a relaxing hour.

Make a poultice from the lightly beaten white of an egg. Bandage the poultice on the closed eyes and leave it there overnight. There should be a big improvement next morning. Cottage cheese in place of egg white is also effective.

‡Colds, Etc.

‡ COLDS

Soon after we completed our first *Chicken Soup* folk remedy book, the respected Mayo Clinic printed the following in their Health Letter:

> There is now evidence that our ancestors may have known more about how to treat sniffles than we do. And that should not be surprising. Indeed, scientific study of folk medicines and cures often has proved to be remarkably rewarding.
>
> Moses Maimonides, a twelfth-century Jewish physician and philosopher, reported that chicken soup is an effective medication as well as a tasty food.
>
> A report published in *Chest*, a medical journal for chest specialists, indicates that hot chicken soup is more effective than other hot liquids in clearing mucus particles from the nose. The cause of this beneficial effect is still not fully understood, but the soup does seem to contain a substance which prompts clearing of nasal mucus. And removal of nasal secretions containing viruses and bacteria is an important part of our body's defense against upper respiratory infections. The study gives sci-

entific respectability to the long-standing conten-
tion that chicken soup might help relieve a head
cold.

Chicken soup—particularly the homemade variety—is a safe, effective treatment for many "self-
limiting" illnesses (those not requiring professional
attention). It is inexpensive and widely available.
Side effects are few, with the notable exception of
weight gain if it is used excessively. (Most canned
chicken soups contain a considerable amount of
salt and should be avoided by people on salt-re-
stricted diets.)

What does it all add up to? Specifically, this
recommendation: Next time you come down with
a head cold, try hot homemade chicken soup before
heading for the pharmacy. We believe chicken soup
can be an excellent treatment for uncomplicated
head colds and other viral respiratory infections for
which antibiotics ordinarily are not helpful. Soup
is less expensive and, most significantly, it carries
little, if any, risk of allergic reactions or other un-
desireable side effects.

We rest our case!

Next to chicken soup, zinc gluconate lozenges are
the most effective cold remedy we've found. In some
cases, it nips the cold in the bud and in other cases, it
considerably shortens the duration of the cold. Please
be sure to follow the dosage carefully: Adults, take 2
lozenges (23 mg each) at the outset and then 1 every
2 hours thereafter, but not more than 12 a day, and for
no longer than 2 days. Got it? Also, do not take them
on an empty stomach. Even if you don't feel like eating,

consume half a fruit before you take a lozenge. Suck
on the lozenge so that it comes in prolonged contact
with your mouth and throat. Honey-flavored are the
best; lemon are the pits. Zinc gluconate also comes in
46 mg tablets. If you get them instead of the 23 mg,
take 1 at the outset and 1 every 4 hours, not exceeding
6 a day.

For teenage and children's dosages, see "Infants and
Children."

The second you feel a cold coming on, take 1 teaspoonful of oil of eucalyptus, hold it in your mouth for
10 minutes, then swallow it. It has been known to stop
a cold from progressing.

Germs seem to attack the weakest part of the body.
Is that why we all get head colds?

When you have a head cold and the excessive mucus
that's part of it, sleeping with a small piece of carrot in
each nostril is said to dislodge the mucus.

Another popular remedy, similar to the one above,
also for a head cold, is to cut 2 thin-as-can-be strips of

orange rind. Roll them up with the white spongy part (the pith) on the outside, and stick one in each nostril. Stay that way until your head cold is better, or you can't stand the rind in your nostrils anymore, whichever comes first. Be sure to leave orange rind sticking out of your nose so you can dislodge it easily.

The first of our 5 senses to develop is our sense of smell. Eventually, the average human nose can recognize 10,000 different odors, but not when we have a head cold. To clear the head and stop a runny nose, begin by cutting the crust off a piece of bread. Plug in your iron to "hot"—wool or cotton setting. Carefully iron the bread crust. When it starts to burn, lift the iron off the crust and cautiously inhale the smoke through your nostrils for 2 minutes. Repeat this procedure 3 times throughout the day. We've been told that the runny nose stops and the head cold clears up in a very short time, 1 or 2 days.

Before bedtime, take a ginger bath and sweat away your cold overnight. Put 3 tablespoonsful of grated ginger root in a stocking and knot the stocking closed. Throw it into a hot bath, along with the contents of a 2-ounce container of powdered ginger. Stir the bath water with a wooden spoon. Then, get in and soak for 10 to 15 minutes. Once you're out of the tub, dry yourself thoroughly, preferably with a rough towel. Put on warm sleep clothes and cover your head with a towel or woolen scarf, leaving just your face exposed. Get in bed, under the covers and go to sleep. If you perspire enough to feel uncomfortably wet, change into dry sleepwear during the night.

Talk about "sweating it out," (as we did above), a gem therapist told us that wearing a topaz activates body heat and, therefore, helps cure ailments that may benefit from increased perspiration.

In our first folk remedy book, we talked about the effectiveness of garlic for a cold. The onion, a member of the same family, is also a popular folk medicine for colds. Here are some ways in which the onion is used:

• Cut an onion in half and place the 2 halves on each side of your bed so you can inhale the fumes as you sleep.
• Eat a whole onion before bedtime in order to break up the cold overnight.
• Dip a slice of raw onion in a glass of hot water. After a few seconds, remove the onion and, when the water cools, start sipping it, and continue to do so throughout the day.
• If you like your onions fried, take the hot fried onions, put them in a flannel or woolen cloth and bind them on your chest overnight.
• Putting slices of raw onion on the soles of one's feet, and holding the slices in place with woolen socks, is thought to draw out infection and fever by morning.

‡ FLU
The second you feel fluish, take 1 tablespoonful of liquid lecithin. And continue to take 1 tablespoonful every 8 hours for the next 2 days. Some naturalists

believe that these large doses of lecithin may prevent a viral flu from flourishing.

This formula was handed down from generation to generation by a family who tells of the many lives it saved during the 1918 flu epidemic in Stuttgart, Germany. They claim that this elixir cleans the harmful bacteria out of the blood.

Peel and cut ½ pound of garlic into small pieces. Put the garlic and 1 quart of cognac (90 proof) in a dark brown bottle. Seal it airtight with paraffin wax or tape. During the day, keep the bottle in the sun or other light, warm place like in the kitchen near the oven. At night, move the bottle from the light, warm place to a dark, cool place. After 14 days and nights, open the bottle and strain. Put the strained elixir back in the bottle. It is now ready to be used. The potency of this mixture is said to last one year, so label the bottle with the expiration date accordingly.

If you already have the flu, take 20 drops of the formula, with a glass of water, 1 hour before each meal (3 times a day), for 5 days.

To prevent the flu, take 10 to 15 drops with a glass of water, 1 hour before each meal, daily.

‡ HAY FEVER

March brings April showers. April showers bring May flowers. May flowers bring hay fever.

To subdue the symptoms of hay fever, folk medicine practitioners had their patients smoke coffee grounds in a pipe and inhale the smoke.

‡ HAY FEVER PREVENTION

Starting in March and continuing to the beginning of June, drink 1 cup of fenugreek seed tea a day. This remedy goes back to the ancient Egyptians and forward to Armenian mountaineers who drink 1 cup of fenugreek tea before each meal to clear and stimulate their senses of smell and taste.

‡ ALLERGIES

There are almost as many types of allergies as there are people who have them. Obviously, allergies need to be handled on a one-on-one basis. We found a few healthful hints that just may help the allergy sufferer:

It is said that there are chemicals in bananas that repel allergies, that is, unless you're allergic to bananas.

Vitamin-rich watercress is said to be an antiallergen. Eat it in salads, sandwiches and sauces. It's potent stuff, so eat small portions of it at a time.

We were told that licorice helps build up an immunity to allergens. Add 3 ounces of cut licorice root (see

"Sources") to 1 quart of water. Boil it for 10 minutes in an enamel or glass pot, then strain into a bottle.

DOSE: 1 tablespoonful before each meal, every other day until you've taken the licorice root water for 6 days. By then, we hope, it will make a difference in terms of your resistance to allergies.

‡Constipation

You are most likely reading this page because you're seeking a natural laxative. Therefore, you may already know that some of the commercial chemical laxatives can kill friendly bacteria; lessen the absorption of nutrients and get rid of necessary vitamins; stuff up the intestinal walls, turn users into addicts and eventually *cause* constipation.

We offer easy-to-take, inexpensive, nonchemical constipation relievers that should not present any problem side effects if taken in moderation, using good common sense.

If, after trying these remedies, you still have a persisting problem, you should see a health professional.

Take 2 small beets, scrub them clean and eat them in the morning. You should have a bowel movement 12 hours later.

Flaxseed is a popular folk treatment for constipation. Take 1 to 2 tablespoonsful with lots of water right after lunch or dinner.

Sunflower seeds are filled with health-giving properties and have also been known to promote regularity. Eat a handful of the shelled, raw and unsalted seeds every day.

For those of you who feel you need a good colon cleansing, drink an 8-ounce glass of warm sauerkraut juice and then an 8-ounce glass of grapefruit juice (unsweetened)—one right after the other. It should do the job. Okay, so it may rip your throat out in the process.

Eat at least 3 raw fruits a day. One of the 3, preferably an apple, should be eaten 2 hours after dinner.

We were told about an acupressure technique that is supposed to encourage a complete evacuation of the bowels in 15 minutes. For 3 to 5 minutes, massage the area underneath your lower lip, in the middle of your chin. (We call this the "Kirk Douglas look-alike remedy.")

The findings of recent studies say that monounsaturated fatty acid—the kind found in olive oil—is best for lowering cholesterol levels. Olive oil is also a help when a laxative is needed. Take 1 tablespoonful in the morning and 1 tablespoonful an hour after eating dinner.

For some people, brewer's yeast does the trick. One man we heard about regulated himself by taking 1 heaping teaspoonful of brewer's yeast and 1 heaping teaspoonful of wheat germ with each meal.

Start with small amounts of either or both brewer's

yeast and wheat germ. Gradually increase your intake and stop when the amount you're taking works for you.

Are persimmons in season? Try one. It's been known to relieve constipation.

For a mild laxative, soak six dates in a glass of hot water. When the water is cool, drink it, then eat the dates.

‡Coughs

‡ COUGHS IN GENERAL

Peel and slice a large turnip. Spread honey between all the slices and let it stand for several hours while the turnip/honey syrup oozes out and collects at the bottom of the dish. Whenever the cough acts up, take a teaspoonful of the syrup.

Add ½ cup of raw, shelled and unsalted sunflower seeds to 5 cups of water and boil in an enamel or glass pot until the water is reduced to about 2 cups. Strain, then stir in ¾ cup of gin and ½ cup of honey. Mix well and bottle it. Take 1 to 2 teaspoonsful 4 times a day.

Licorice root contains saponins, natural substances known to break up and loosen mucus. When you have a hacking cough, drink a cup of licorice root tea (see "Sources").

An acupressure joint that has been known to stop a cough is the one near the end of the middle finger. With the fingers of your right hand, squeeze the top joint of the left hand's middle finger. Keep squeezing until you stop wheezing.

This bean purée remedy is for one of those mean, down-deep coughs that nothing seems to reach. Put a cupful of kidney beans in a strainer and wash them off. Then, put them in water and let them soak overnight (while you probably cough your head off, right?). Next morning, drain the beans, tie them up in a clean cloth and bruise them—pound them with a blunt object like a rolling pin, frying pan or hammer. Place the bruised—uh, battered beans in an enamel or glass saucepan with 3 cloves of peeled and minced garlic and 2 cups of water. Bring the mixture to a boil, then simmer for 1½ to 2 hours, until tender. Add more water if necessary. Take 1 tablespoonful of this bean purée the second your cough acts up. This is the Rambo of cough remedies!

‡ BRONCHIAL COUGHS

Add 3 drops of oil of fennel and 3 drops of oil of anise to 6 tablespoonsful of honey. Shake vigorously and bottle it. Take 1 teaspoonful when you start to cough. If you haven't prepared the syrup in advance of your cough and now that you need it, you don't have the necessary ingredients, you may want to settle for second best. Do you have the liqueur called anisette? Take 1 teaspoonful of anisette in 1 tablespoon of hot water every 3 hours.

This Japanese remedy is said to be beneficial for bronchitis sufferers. Combine a raw egg with 2 ounces of sake (Japanese liquor made from fermented rice) in an enamel or glass pan and bring it to a boil. As soon as it cools, drink it—but not on an empty stomach. This drink has a warming effect since it stimulates circulation.

Put 4 minced cloves of garlic and an equal amount of petroleum jelly in an enamel or glass pan over a low fire. Stir the mixture until the petroleum jelly is melted. Once the mixture cools, massage this garlicky paste into the chest and back to help clear up the congestion.

‡ TICKLING COUGH
Many people are bothered by a tickling type cough, usually at night in their sleep. Put 2 teaspoonsful of apple cider vinegar in a glass of water and keep it by your bedside. When the "tickling" wakes you up, swallow 1 or 2 mouthfuls of the vinegar water and go back to a restful sleep.

‡ WHOOPING COUGH
A Russian folk remedy for whooping cough is to massage the spine with garlic. For an easy way to do this, see the last remedy under "Bronchial Coughs."

‡ SMOKER'S COUGH

This remedy is updated form the *1888 Universal Cookery Book*. Pour 1 quart of boiling water over 4 tablespoonsful of whole flaxseed and steep for 3 hours. Strain, add the juice of 2 lemons and sweeten with honey (which replaces the crystals of rock candy used in the original remedy). Take a tablespoonful when the cough acts up.

An even better remedy for smoker's cough . . . STOP SMOKING!

‡Diarrhea

Diarrhea is a common condition usually caused by overeating, or a minor bacterial infection, or mild food poisoning, and sometimes by emotional anxiety or extreme fatigue.

Even a quick and simple bout of diarrhea depletes the system of potassium and magnesium, often leaving the sufferer tired, dehydrated and depressed. It's important to keep drinking during and after a siege in order to avoid depletion and dehydration.

NOTE: If diarrhea persists, it may be a symptom of a more serious ailment. Seek professional medical attention.

A West Indies remedy for diarrhea is a pinch of allspice in a cup of warm water or milk. A Pennsylvania Dutch remedy is 2 pinches of cinnamon in a cup of warm milk. A Brazilian remedy calls for 2 pinches of cinnamon and 1 pinch of powdered cloves in a cup of warm milk.

We may as well "milk" this for all it's worth with a Welsh remedy that requires a cup of boiled milk and a red-hot fireplace poker. Carefully place the red-hot poker into the cup of milk. Keep it there for 30 seconds. The poker supposedly charges the milk with iron which is a homeopathic treatment of diarrhea. Drink the iron-charged milk slowly.

The combination of cinnamon and cayenne pepper is known to be very effective in tightening the bowels very quickly. In fact, it probably takes longer to prepare the tea than for it to work.

Bring 2 cups of water to a boil, then add ¼ teaspoonful of cinnamon and ⅛ teaspoonful of cayenne pepper. Let the mixture simmer for 20 minutes. As soon as it's cool enough to drink, have ¼ cupful every half hour.

Add 1 teaspoonful of powdered ginger root to 1 cup of just-boiled water. To control diarrhea, drink 3 cups of the mixture throughout the day.

Grate an onion and squeeze it through cheesecloth so you get 2 tablespoonsful (1 ounce) onion juice. Take 2 tablespoonsful of onion juice every hour, along with 1 cup of peppermint tea.

An adsorbent (that's right, *ad*sorbent) substance attaches things to its surface instead of absorbing them into itself. Activated charcoal is the most powerful adsorbent known. Charcoal capsules or tablets can help stop diarrhea quickly by adsorbing the enterobacteria or toxins that may cause the problem. Follow the instructions on the box.

NOTE: Be sure to heed the warning and drug interaction precaution. Activated charcoal is not for everyday use, as it adsorbs the vitamins and minerals you need to be healthy.

If you don't have charcoal tablets or capsules, you might try eating a slice or 2 of burnt (charred) toast.

Raspberry leaf tea is a popular folk remedy for children and adults. Combine 1 ounce of dried raspberry leaves with 2 cups of water (a piece of cinnamon stick is optional), and simmer in an enamel or glass saucepan for 25 minutes. Strain, cool and drink throughout the day.

According to Hippocrates, the father of medicine, everyone should drink barley water daily to maintain good health.

One of the benefits is its effectiveness in treating diarrhea. Boil 2 ounces of pearled barley in 6 cups of water until there's about one half the water—3 cups—left in the pot. Strain. If necessary, add honey and lemon to taste. Not only should you drink the barley water throughout the day, you should also eat the barley.

The navel is an acupressure point for treating diarrhea. Using your thumb or the heel of your hand, press in and massage the area in a circular motion for about 2 minutes.

‡ DYSENTERY

All of the above "diarrhea" remedies may help treat bacterial dysentery. However, amoebic dysentery (caused by amoeba living in the raw green vegetables of some countries) and viral dysentery are more severe forms of dysentery and should be treated by a health professional.

‡Ears

‡ EARACHES

Fill the ear with three warm (not too hot) drops of olive oil and plug the ear with a puff of cotton. Do this 3 or 4 times a day until the earache is gone.

This remedy is a little more complex but might provide faster relief than the one above. Mix the juice from grated fresh ginger with an equal amount of sesame oil. Drop in 3 drops of the mixture and plug the ear with a puff of cotton. Keep it there for a few hours.

This reflexology remedy requires something sterile and hard to bite down on. The ideal thing is one of those cotton cylinders the dentist uses. What we do is wad up a piece of cheesecloth and it works fine. Place the wad of whatever in back of the last tooth on the side of the aching ear, and bite down on it for 5 minutes. This stimulates the pressure point that goes directly to the ear. Repeat this procedure every 2 hours until the earache is gone. This acupressure process relieves the pain of an earache and has been known to improve hearing as well.

Another effective way of easing the pain of an earache is with a soothing camomile poultice. If you don't have the loose herb, use a couple of tea bags instead (see "Preparation Guide").

Cut a large onion in half. Take out the inside of the onion so that the remaining part will fit over your ear. Warm the onion "earmuff" in the oven, then put it over your ear. It should help draw out the pain.

‡ RUNNING EAR INFECTION

You'll need to go to a good old-fashioned Italian fish store for this remedy. Get the soft transparent bone from a squid. Bake it and crush it into a black powder. Taken orally, ½ teaspoonful before breakfast and another ½ teaspoonful before dinner, it is said to help clear up a running ear infection.

‡ "SWIMMER'S EAR" PREVENTION

A lot of people seem to be plagued by recurrent painful ear-canal infections soon after swimming. Here's a solution that may prevent infections: Add 1 teaspoonful of white vinegar to 4 tablespoonsful (2 ounces) of just-boiled water. Once the liquid is cool, store it in a bottle. Right after swimming put 2 drops of the vinegar mixture in each ear.

‡ GETTING THE WAX OUT

Wax build-up? Warm 2 teaspoonsful of sesame oil and put a spoonful in each ear. Be sure the oil is not too hot. Gently plug the ear with a puff of cotton, and allow the oil to float around for a while. Once the sesame oil softens the wax, you can wash out the ears completely. The results: no more oil, no more wax.

‡ EARLOBE INFECTION

Men as well as women have been troubled with earlobe infections from ear-piercing. Put castor oil on your lobes a few times a day—the more the better. The infection should clear up in 2 or 3 days at most.

‡ RINGING (TINNITUS)

We heard about a woman who had constant ringing in her ears for years. None of the specialists could help her. As a last resort, she started using castor oil. After a month, the ringing subsided considerably. Within 3 months, it was completely gone.

If your ringing or buzzing is not caused by medication you're taking, and if your doctor doesn't know what it's from or what to do for it, you might want to try castor oil—3 or 4 drops a day in each ear. To get full benefit from the castor oil, plug the ear with cotton once you've put in the drops.

‡ PARTIAL LOSS OF HEARING

A loud noise, a cold or wax buildup can cause partial loss of hearing. In Sicily, where garlic is a cure-all, they stew a few cloves in olive oil, then press it and strain it. On a daily basis, 3 or 4 drops of the garlic/olive oil juice is placed in the ear(s) and plugged up with cotton. It is said to restore one's hearing.

"Hey, I can hear now."
"Good. I've been wanting to tell you something: YOU SMELL OF GARLIC!"

‡Emphysema

If you've been diagnosed as having the lung condition known as emphysema, and you're still smoking cigarettes, we don't want to know from you! Don't bother reading any more. Turn to the "Smoke Stoppers" chapter. Come back when you've stopped smoking.

Now then, combine ½ teaspoonful of raw honey with 5 drops of anise oil and take this dosage a half hour before each meal.

We've heard positive reports about this remedy. It's worth a try.

When you're having a hard time breathing, sit down, lean forward and put your elbows on your knees. This position can make breathing easier because it elevates the diaphragm, which is your muscle of breathing.

‡Eyes

‡ CINDERS

When something gets in your eye, try not to rub the eye. You'll irritate it, then it's hard to tell whether or not the foreign particle is out.

Get a tissue ready. With one hand pull your lashes so that the upper lid is away from your eye. With the other hand, appropriately position the tissue in the center of your face and blow your nose 3 times.

If the remedy above didn't work for you and you have access to a kitchen, put some pure olive oil in a teaspoon, hold a lit match under it for a few seconds—long enough to *slightly* warm the oil. Then put 2 drops in the eye that has the particle. What? You don't have an eyedropper? Buy one at any health food store or pharmacy and keep it in your medicine chest for just such occasions.

Until you get an eyedropper for the above remedy, you may want to try this: 1 drop of fresh lemon juice (1 drop only!) in 1 ounce of warm water and wash your eye with it. It should remove the particle and it is surprisingly soothing.

‡ IRRITATIONS

If your eyes are irritated from a foreign particle, cooking fumes, cigarette smoke, dust, etc., put 2 drops of castor oil in each eye, or 2 drops of milk in each eye.

Use any of the "Eyewashes" listed at the end of this chapter.

‡ BLOODSHOT EYES

If you don't drink in excess and you get enough sleep, but still have bloodshot eyes on a regular basis, you may be bothered by your contacts, allergic to the eye makeup you wear, or you may be deficient in vitamin B-2 (riboflavin). Take 15 mg of B-2 daily. You might also want to have a tablespoonful of brewer's yeast every day.

Use any of the "Eyewashes" listed at the end of this chapter and you might want to try the grated potato remedy listed under "Black Eye."

‡ STIES

Roasted bancha tea bags are available at most health food stores. Steep a tea bag in hot water for 10 minutes and add 1 teaspoonful of sea salt (available at health food stores as well as supermarkets). Saturate a cotton pad in the lukewarm liquid and apply it to your closed eye, keeping it there for 10 minutes at a time, 3 times a day.

Some sty sufferers have had great success by gently applying castor oil to the problem area. In addition to, or instead of, the above remedy, dab on some castor oil several times throughout the day until the sty disappears.

‡ STY PREVENTION

Lydia went to school with a girl named Madeline whose nickname was "Sty." She always seemed to have a sty coming or going. If you're like Madeline and are prone to sties, prepare a strong cup of burdock seed tea or ground centaury plant tea every morning and take 1 tablespoonful before each meal and 1 at bedtime (see "Sources" and "Preparation Guide").

‡ CATARACTS

There are amazing new surgical procedures now for removing cataracts. Know your options. While you're investigating the alternatives, you might want to try one of the following:

Honey! No, we're not getting overly friendly here, we're just relaying a remedy to help restore the eyesight of people with cataracts. (See "Night Blindess" for details.)

Dr. Gladys of the Association for Research and Enlightenment Clinic of Phoenix, Arizona, recommends 2 drops of castor oil in each eye at bedtime. If there is no improvement after a month, other therapists suggest that 1 drop of linseed oil (found in drugstores) in each eye every night, be used instead. But start with the castor oil and stay with it for a month.

Noted English physician Nicholas Culpeper was a great believer in the healing effects of camomile eyewashes to improve a cataract condition. (See "Eyewashes" at the end of this chapter.)

Research scientists have found that a deficiency of vitamin B-2 (riboflavin) can cause cataracts. Tests done at the University of Georgia Hospital have built a most impressive case for B-2 preventing cataracts as well as clearing up existing conditions. Brewer's yeast is the source richest in riboflavin. Take 1 tablespoonful a day and/or 15 mg of vitamin B-2. Along with a B-2 vitamin, take a B-complex vitamin to avoid high urinary losses of B vitamins.

‡ CATARACT PREVENTION
See the above vitamin B-2 remedy.

‡ EYESTRAIN (TIRED EYES)
If your eyes are strained and tired, chances are the rest of your body is also dragging. Lie down with your feet raised higher than your head. Relax that way for about 15 minutes. This gravity-reversing process should make you and your eyes feel refreshed and rarin' to go.

Cut 2 thin slices of a raw red potato and keep them on your closed eyelids for at least 20 minutes. Red potatoes are said to have more healing energy, but any other potato will work, too.

Steep rosemary in hot water for 10 minutes. (That line sounds like a recipe for a soap opera.) Use a rosemary tea bag or 1 teaspoonful of the loose herb to a cup of just-boiled water. Saturate a cotton pad with the tea and keep it on your eyes for 15 minutes. Rosemary should help draw out that tired-eye feeling.

Also, see "Palming"—the last remedy under "Vision Improvers."

‡ EYESTRAIN PREVENTION
Looking at red ink on white paper for long periods of time can cause eyestrain and headaches. Stay out of the red!

‡ BLACK EYE
Pour witch hazel on a cotton pad and apply it to the bruised, closed eye. Lie down with your feet slightly

higher than your head for a half hour while the witch hazel stays in place.

Walk into a door, did you? I hope it was the door to the kitchen. If you're there now, peel and grate a potato (a red potato is best). Make a poultice out of it (see "Preparation Guide") and put it on the black eye for 20 minutes. The cliché of a beefsteak on a shiner came about because of the potassium in the meat. Potassium chloride is one of the most effective healing compounds, and potatoes are the best source of potassium chloride.

This remedy is also beneficial for bloodshot eyes.

‡ EYE TWITCH

Pressure and tension can cause eyelid twitching. Aside from the 2-week vacation you should take, eat calcium-rich foods. According to some nutritionists, adults can and should get all the calcium we require through non-dairy foods: green vegetables, sesame seeds, whole grains, unrefined cereals, salmon and sardines.

‡ INFLAMED EYES AND EYELIDS

Crush a tablespoonful of fennel seeds and add it to a pint of just-boiled water. Let it steep for 15 minutes, then dunk cotton pads in the liquid and place it over your eyelids for about 15 minutes.

There's an herb called horsetail (see "Sources"). Steep 1 teaspoonful of dried horsetail in hot water for 10 minutes. Saturate cotton pads with it and apply the pads to your eyelids for 10 minutes. Redunk the pads in the liquid, then keep them on your eyes for another

10 minutes. One more time! After half an hour, the inflammation should start calming down.

Freshly sliced cucumber on eyelids for about 15 minutes is soothing and healing. You may also peel the cucumber and squeeze a couple of drops of juice directly into each eye.

Also, use any of the "Eyewashes" listed at the end of this chapter. Try "Palming," too. It's the last remedy under "Vision Improvers."

‡ CONJUNCTIVITIS (PINKEYE)
The plant, eyebright, is particularly effective in the treatment of conjunctivitis. Add 3 drops of tincture of eyebright (available at health food stores) to a tablespoonful of boiled water. When cool enough to use, bathe the eye in the mixture. Since this condition is a contagious one, wash the eyecup thoroughly after you've washed one eye, then mix a new batch of eyebright with water and wash the other eye. Do this 3 or 4 times a day until the condition clears up. Or, use the "Eyewashes" listed at the end of this chapter.

Goat milk yogurt can help clear up this uncomfortable condition. Apply a yogurt poultice to the infected eye(s) daily. Also, eat a portion or 2 of the yogurt each day. The active culture in yogurt can help destroy the infection-causing bacteria in your system.

‡ NIGHT BLINDNESS

Since this remedy seems so yucky, we would not have included it had we not heard of the wonderful results from several reliable sources. Every day for 2 weeks, put a drop of raw honey in each eye. (We said "yucky" didn't we?) It stings like crazy for a few seconds until tears wash away the pain. Within a week or 2 there should be a noticeable improvement in your night vision.

Try "Palming." It's the last remedy under "Vision Improvers."

‡ SUN BLINDNESS

Sun blindness is caused by exposure to large expanses of snow or ice for a considerable length of time. For this condition, make a poultice from the lightly beaten white of an egg. Bandage the poultice on the closed eyes and sleep that way. There should be a big improvement next morning. Cottage cheese or raw veal in place of egg white is also effective.

‡ SUN BLINDNESS PREVENTION

Skiers will find this remedy most helpful in coping with large expanses of snow. Eat a handful of sunflower seeds every day. (Buy them shelled, raw and unsalted.) Within no time, the eyes may have a much easier time adjusting to the brightness of the snow, thanks to the sunflower seeds.

‡ VISION IMPROVERS

You know all the talk about carrots being good for your eyes? They are! Drink 5 to 6 ounces of fresh carrot juice twice a day for at least 2 weeks. Obviously, you'll need a juicer or a nearby juice bar. After the 2 weeks, ease off to 1 glass of carrot juice a day . . . forever!

According to J. I. Rodale, founder of *Prevention Magazine*, sunflower seeds are a miracle food. We agree. Eat a handful (shelled, raw and unsalted) every day.

Foods rich in vitamin A should be eaten regularly for your entire body as well as for your eyes. Some of those foods are: parsley, sweet potato or yam, endive, beet greens, chard leaves.

We've heard that wearing a gold earring in your left ear improves and preserves one's eyesight. We weren't going to include this as a remedy because we thought it's a useless superstition. Then we read in David Louis' book, *2201 Fascinating Facts* that pirates believed that piercing their ears and wearing earrings improved their eyesight—and the swashbucklers may have been right. The idea, which had been scoffed at for centuries, has been reevaluated in light of recent acupuncture theory, which holds that the point of the lobe where the ear is pierced is the same acupuncture point that controls the eyes.

Hmmmm. Get out the gold earrings.

We've thoroughly researched "palming" and no two of our resources agree on the procedure. We'll give you a couple of variations. Test them and see what works for you.

Sit. (They all agree on that.) Rub your hands together until you feel heat. With your elbows on the table, place the heels of your hands over your eyes, blocking out all light. Some feel it's better to keep one's eyes open in the dark; others advocate closed eyes. The length of time to sit this way also ranges—from 2 minutes to 10 minutes.

Eyes opened or closed, any length of time, "palming" is beneficial for improving vision, for nearsightedness, tired eyes, astigmatisms, inflammations and may even help squinters.

‡ GLAUCOMA

Vitamin B-2 (riboflavin) deficiency is one of the most common vitamin deficiencies in this country. It's also the vitamin that's most beneficial for eye problems such as glaucoma. Take 100 mg daily, along with a B-complex. The reason for the B-complex is that large doses of any one of the B vitamins can result in urinary losses of other B vitamins.

Bathe the eyes mornings and evenings with fennel seed, camomile or eyebright. (See "Eyewashes" for directions.)

NOTE: Glaucoma is a serious condition. When using any home remedy, be sure it's under the supervision of an eye specialist.

‡ EYEWASHES
Commercial eyedrops eliminate the redness because of a decongestant that constricts the blood vessels. Using these drops on a regular basis can worsen the problem. The blood vessels will enlarge again in less and less time. Make your own eyedrops from the following herbs, or just bathe your eyes with these eyewashes:

‡ Eyebright
To make an eyebright eyewash, add 1 ounce of the whole dried herb, eyebright, to 1 pint of just-boiled water and let it steep for 10 minutes. Strain the mixture thoroughly through a superfine strainer or through unbleached muslin. Wait until it's cool enough to use.

Or, add 3 drops of tincture of eyebright to a tablespoonful of boiled water, and, again, wait until it's cool enough to use.

‡ Camomile
Add 1 teaspoonful of dried camomile flowers to 1 cup of just-boiled water. Steep for 5 minutes and strain the mixture thoroughly, through a superfine strainer or through unbleached muslin. Wait until it's cool enough to use.

Or, add 12 drops of tincture of camomile to 1 cup of just-boiled water.

‡ Fennel Seeds

Add 1 teaspoonful of crushed fennel seeds to 1 cup of just-boiled water. Steep for 5 minutes and strain the mixture thoroughly through a superfine strainer or through unbleached muslin. Wait until it's cool enough to use.

‡ Sunburned Eyes and Eyelids (See: "Burns.")

‡ EYEGLASS WEARERS

To avoid streaks on your eyeglass lenses, clean them with a touch of vinegar or vodka.

‡Fainting Prevention

When you feel as though you're going to faint, sit down and put your head between your knees. If you're in an appropriate place, lie down with your feet and torso elevated so that your head is lower than your heart. That's the secret of preventing a faint—getting your head lower than your heart so the blood can rush to your brain.

In India, instead of smelling salts people take a couple of strong whiffs of half an onion to bring them around.

If it's a scorcher of a day and you're feeling every degree of it, or if you're in a very warm room that's making you feel faint, just run cold tap water over the insides of your wrists. If there are ice cubes around, rub them on your wrists. Relief is almost immediate.

A friend of ours is a paramedic. When one of her patients is about to faint, she pinches the fleshy part between the patient's upper lip and nose, and prevents the faint from happening.

If you have frequent fainting spells, we suggest you consult a health professional. They can be a *symptom* of an ailment.

‡Fatigue

‡ PICKER-UPPERS

A Chinese theory is that "tiredness" collects on the insides of one's elbows and the backs of one's knees. Wake up your body by slapping both those areas.

Tough day at the office? Need to get that second wind? Ready for a drink? Tired of all these questions? Add 1 tablespoonful of blackstrap molasses to a glass of milk and bottoms up.

Call on your imagination for this visualization exercise. Sit up with your arms over your head and your palms facing the ceiling. With your right hand, pluck a fistful of vitality out of the air. Next, let your left hand grab its share. Open both hands, allowing all that energy to flow down your arms to your neck, shoulders and chest. Start over again. This time, when you open your hands, let the energy flow straight down to your waist, hips, thighs, legs, feet and toes. There! You've revitalized your body. Now stand up feeling refreshed.

A bunch of grapes can give you a bunch of energy. Hey, maybe that's why you always see pictures of people eating grapes at those bacchanalian orgies.

When you just can't keep your eyes open or your head up and you don't know how you'll make it to the end of the day at your office, run away from it all. Go to the bathroom or a secluded spot and run in place. Don't overdo it. Run for 2 minutes and you'll keep going the rest of the day.

‡ STAMINA

Three cheers for chia. According to a study of American Indians, a pinch of chia seeds helped the braves brave their arduous around-the-clock days of hunting. Ground chia seeds, available at health food stores, can be sprinkled on salads or in soup for those on-the-go, around-the-clock days when stamina counts.

‡ START YOUR DAY
THE ENERGY WAY

Here's how to wake up your metabolism in the morning: squeeze out the juice of half a grapefruit into a glass. Fill the rest of the glass with warm water. Drink it down slowly, then eat the fruit of the squeezed-out half grapefruit. Now that your thyroid is activated, have a nice day!

If, after a full night's sleep, you get up feeling sluggish, it may be due to a tired liver. Stand up. Place your right hand above your waist, on the bottom of your ribs on your right side, with your fingers apart, pointing towards your left side. Place your left hand the same way on your left side. Ready? You press your right hand in, then back in place. You press your left hand in, then back in place. You do the Hokey-Pokey and you turn your—No! Sorry, I got carried away. Now then, press your right hand in, then back in place. Press your left hand in, then back in place. Do it a dozen times on each side when you get up each morning. In a couple of weeks, this liver massage may make a big difference in your daily energy level. Cutting out heavy starches and sweets from your diet can also go a long way in adding to your get-up-and-go.

‡ MENTAL ALERTNESS

We've read case histories where, within weeks, the intake of pollen has not only increased a person's physical energy, but restored mental alertness and eliminated lapses of memory and confusion. Suggested dosage: 1 teaspoonful of the granular pollen after breakfast, or two 500 mg pollen pills after breakfast.

‡Feet, Ankles and Legs

"Ow! Do my shoes hurt me!"
"No wonder your shoes hurt you. You have them on the wrong feet."
"But I don't have any other feet."

We *don't* have any other feet. That's why we should take care of the ones we have.

According to podiatrist Dr. Steven Baff, 40 percent of American children develop foot ailments by age six and, by adulthood, 80 percent of Americans suffer from foot problems.

Here are some remedies:

‡ CORNS

Make a paste out of 1 teaspoonful of brewer's yeast and a few drops of lemon juice. Spread the mixture on a cotton pad and apply it to the corn, binding it in place, and leaving it overnight. Change the dressing daily until the corn is gone.

A paste of powdered chalk and water should also take care of the corn.

A Hawaiian medicine man recommends pure papaya juice on a cotton pad, or a piece of papaya pulp directly on the corn. Bind in place and leave it on overnight. Change daily until the corn is gone.

Australian shepherds squeeze the juice from the stems of dandelions and apply it to the corn every day until the corn disappears, usually within a week.

‡ TIRED, SORE, BURNING—
OH, YOUR ACHING FEET!

This remedy requires 2 basins or dishpans. Fill 1 with ½ cup Epsom salts and about 1 gallon of hot (not scalding) water; fill the other basin with ice cubes. Sit down with a watch or timer. Put your feet in the hot water for one minute and then in the ice cubes for half a minute. Alternate back and forth for about 10 minutes. Your feet will feel better. This procedure also helps regulate high blood pressure, may prevent varicose veins, improves circulation and, by doing it on a regular basis, a chronic "cold feet" condition may be eliminated.

A modified version of the above is: Stand in the bathtub and first let hot water run on your feet, then let ice cold water run on your feet, timing it the same as above. DO NOT EXCEED ONE (1) MINUTE OF HOT OR COLD WATER ON YOUR FEET!

Add 1 cup of apple cider vinegar to a basin of lukewarm water. Then soak your feet in it for at least 15 minutes. The heat and hurt should be gone by then. Will you save me a dance?

Boil or roast a large turnip until it's nice and soft. Then mash it and spread half of it on a white cotton handkerchief; spread the other half on another handkerchief. Apply the turnip mush to the bottoms of your bare feet, bandage them in place, and sit with your feet elevated for about half an hour. This sole food should draw out the pain and tiredness.

‡ SWEATY FEET

The average pair of feet gives off about ½ pint of perspiration daily. It's amazing we don't all seem to

slosh around. Well, for those of you who feel like you
do . . .

Put some bran or uncooked oat flakes into your socks.
It should absorb the sweat and make you feel more
comfortable. Start conservatively with 1 teaspoonful to
1 tablespoonful, depending on the size of your feet.

‡ ATHLETE'S FOOT

Grate an onion and squeeze it through cheesecloth
to get onion juice. Massage the juice into the fungus-
infected areas of your foot. Leave it on for 10 minutes,
then rinse your foot in lukewarm water and dry it thoroughly. Repeat this procedure 3 times a day until the
condition clears up.

To avoid reinfecting yourself with athlete's foot, soak
your socks and hose in vinegar. Also wipe out your shoes
with vinegar. The smell of vinegar will vanish (say that
3 times fast) after being exposed to the air for about 15
minutes.

‡ CALLUSES

You can soften your calluses by applying any of the
following oils: wheat germ oil, castor oil, sesame seed

oil or olive oil. Apply the oil as often as possible through-out the day, day after day.

Walking barefoot in the sand, particularly wet sand, is wonderful for your feet. It acts as an abrasive and sloughs off dead skin that could lead to corns and cal-luses.

If you're not near the beach (see above remedy), add 1 tablespoonful of baking soda to a basin of lukewarm water and soak your feet in it for 15 minutes. Then take a pumice stone (available at health food stores and pharmacies) and, carefully file away the tough skin.

Cut an onion in half (the size of the onion should be determined by the size of the callused area the onion's cut surface has to cover). Let the onion halves soak in wine vinegar for 4 hours. Then take the onion halves and apply them to the calluses. Bind them in place and leave them overnight. Next morning, you should be able to scrape away the calluses. Don't forget to rinse your feet to get the onion/vinegar smell off.

‡ TOES—TINGLING AND NUMBNESS

Daily doses of 50 mg of vitamin B-6 have been known to eliminate tingling and numbness in toes in about 3 to 4 weeks.

‡ INGROWN TOENAIL

We were surprised to learn that a tendency toward ingrown toenails is inherited.

If you have an ingrown toenail and it's inflamed,

prepare a foot bath by adding 1 ounce of comfrey root to 1 gallon of warm water. Soak your foot in it for 20 minutes.

The nail should be cut straight across, not down into the corners, and not shorter than the toe. You might want a podiatrist to trim the toenail properly. Pay careful attention so you'll be able to take care of your toes yourself and avoid another ingrown nail (and another podiatrist bill).

‡ WEAK ANKLES

This exercise will promote toe flexibility and strengthen the arches as well as the ankles.

Get a dozen marbles and a plastic cup. Put them all on the floor. Pick up each marble with the toes of your right foot and, one by one, drop them in the cup. Then do the same with the toes of your left foot. You may want to add to the fun by timing yourself and seeing if you can keep breaking your previous record. Whatever happens, try not to lose your marbles.

Each night, right before bed, take a raw oyster in the palm of your hand and rub your ankle with it until it just about disintegrates. Then take another raw oyster in the palm of your hand and rub the other ankle. This is supposed to strengthen one's ankles. Why else would you do such a silly thing?

‡ LEG CRAMPS

After doing our homework, we've learned that leg cramps can be caused by a variety of nutritional deficiencies. For instance, calcium. Are you eating lots of greens? (We don't mean *two* olives in your martini.) Cut down on fatty meats, sugar and white flour. In a week, see if you feel a difference.

If you take a diuretic, you may be losing too much potassium from your system. If that's the case, eat a banana or 2 every day. You might also want to ask your doctor to take you off the chemical diuretic and find a natural one, like cucumber, celery or lettuce.

Organic Consumer Report says that muscular cramps that usually occur at night can be relieved within 20 minutes by taking this combination: 1 tablespoonful of calcium lactate, 1 teaspoonful of apple cider vinegar, and 1 teaspoonful of honey in half a glass of warm water.

Vermont's noted doctor, D. C. Jarvis, has a remedy similar to the one above. He suggests 2 teaspoonsful of honey at each meal, or honey combined with 2 teaspoonsful of apple cider vinegar in a glass of water before each meal, helps prevent muscle cramps.

Before you get out of bed in the morning, turn yourself around so that you can put your feet against the wall, higher than your body. Stay that way for 10 minutes. Do the same thing at night, right before you go to sleep. It will improve blood circulation and may prevent muscle cramps.

Lancet, the British medical journal, reports that vitamin E is helpful in relieving cramps in the legs. Take one 100 I.U. of vitamin E before each meal, daily.

Within a week or two there should be a positive difference.

Take advantage of the therapeutic value of a rocking chair. Rock whenever you watch television and for at least 1 hour before bedtime. For those of you who sit most of the time, a rocking chair may prevent varicose veins and blood clots, and improve circulation as well as relieve you of leg cramps.

Drink 1 cup of red raspberry leaf tea in the morning and 1 cup at night. Do this every day and you may no longer have leg cramp attacks.

According to Dr. John M. Ellis, when prescribing vitamin B-6 to his patients (50 mg a day), within 3 weeks the ones suffering from leg cramps were no longer bothered by them. The B-6 also took care of numb and tingling toes.

We were told about a simple technique called "acupinch." It's an acupressure procedure that may help relieve the pain of muscle cramps almost instantly. The second you get a cramp, use your thumb and your index finger and pinch the skin that's between your upper lip and your nose. Keep pinching for about 20 seconds. The pain and cramp should disappear.

Try drinking an 8 ounce glass of water before bedtime.

‡ JOGGER'S LEG CRAMP PREVENTION
Every night, right before going to bed, walk in about 6 inches of cold water in your bathtub for about 3 minutes. The feedback from runners who do this has been very convincing that the cold water walks do prevent leg cramps.

Be sure to have those nonslip stick-ons on the floor of the tub.

‡Female Problems

We've come a long way, baby!

Today, we talk openly about menstruation, pregnancy and menopause, not as sicknesses, but as natural stages of life. We also recognize and deal with premenstrual tension and menopausal irregularities.

We are finally learning to question the male-dominated medical profession after hearing countless stories about hysterectomies, radical mastectomies and other surgery that's sometimes performed whether a woman needs it or not.

Knowledge is power. Television talk shows, bookstores and local libraries are filled with women's health information. Take advantage of these sources so that you can intelligently choose your professional medical care and happily take responsibility for your own body and good health.

Meanwhile, here are some home remedies whispered down from generation to generation.

‡ MENSTRUATION: LIGHTEN THE FLOW

To lighten an unusually heavy menstrual flow, drink yarrow tea— 2 to 3 cups a day until the period is over. To prepare the tea, add 1 or 2 teaspoonsful of dried yarrow (depending on how strong you want the tea to be) to 1 cup of just-boiled water. Let it steep for 10 minutes. Strain and drink.

‡ PROLONGED MENSTRUATION

If you have a history of prolonged periods, get some aduki (a.k.a. azuki) beans and sprout them. Since it takes several days to sprout the beans (see "Preparation Guide"), don't wait until the last minute. Start the process when you're premenstrual. Once the aduki beans have sprouted, eat at least ½ cupful a day. Even if your period is over after the average time of 5, 6 or 7 days, finish the sprouts. They're delicious and rejuvenating, as are most sprouts.

‡ POSTPONED MENSTRUATION

In keeping with the above remedy, and according to a leader of the macrobiotic movement, Michio Kushi, "There is an additional piece of folk knowledge in connection with aduki beans: If a woman wants to postpone her menstruation, she should take 1, 2 or 3 raw aduki beans, without chewing. It has been said that 1 bean will delay the onset 1 day, 2 beans 2 days, and 3 beans 3 days."

(Neither of us would plan a honeymoon by depending on those aduki beans.)

‡ MENSTRUAL CRAMPS

Reduce your salt intake the week before you're expecting your period. It should cut down on the cramps and the bloating.

When it comes to menstrual cramps, how do naturalists spell relief? L-e-a-f-y g-r-e-e-n-s. Eat lots of lettuce, cabbage and parsley before and during your period. To get the full benefit of all vegetables, eat them raw or steamed. Aside from helping reduce crampiness, the leafy greens are diuretics and will relieve you of some bloat.

When your menstrual pains drive you to drink, make that drink some warm gin. Gin is prepared from a mash consisting of 85 percent corn, 12 percent malt, 3 percent rye and distilled in the presence of juniper berries, coriander seeds, etc. Go easy on the gin. You may get rid of the cramps, but you don't want to have to deal with a hangover.

‡ MENSTRUAL IRREGULARITIES

On a daily basis, thoroughly chew, then swallow 1 tablespoonful of sesame seeds. They've been known to regulate menstrual cycles.

‡ MORNING SICKNESS

A doctor at Brigham Young University recommends 2 or 3 capsules of powdered ginger root first thing in the morning to avoid morning sickness.

The doctor also recommends the powdered ginger for motion sickness. You've got it made if you're a pregnant stewardess.

This folk remedy is an oldie and a goodie. Mix ⅓ cup of lime juice and ⅛ teaspoonful of cinnamon in ½ cup of warm water. (It sounds like it could bring on morning sickness.) Drink it as soon as you awaken. It's really known to be quite effective.

‡ QUICK LABOR, EASY DELIVERY AND SPEEDY RECOVERY ("WHO COULD ASK FOR ANYTHING MORE?")

Many sources agree on raspberry tea for the mother-to-be. What our sources don't agree on is when to start drinking the tea. Some say right after conception: "Honey, forget the cigarette, I think I'll have some raspberry tea instead." Some suggest 3 months before delivery and others say 6 weeks before the due date.

The consensus is that pregnant women should drink 2 to 3 cups of raspberry tea a day, starting *at least* 6 weeks before the expected birth.

Add 1 teaspoonful of dried raspberry leaves to 1 cup of just-boiled water. Let it steep for 20 minutes, strain and drink.

‡ BREASTFEEDING

To stimulate milk secretion, drink a mixture of fennel seeds and barley water. Crush 2 tablespoonsful of fennel seeds and simmer them in a quart of barley water (see "Preparation Guide") for 20 minutes. Let it cool and drink it throughout the day.

Peppermint tea is said to increase the supply of mother's milk and it's also known to relieve nervous tension and improve digestion. Drink 2 to 3 cups a day.

Add lentil soup to your diet. You can even sprout lentils (see "Preparation Guide"). They're very rich in calcium and other nutrients necessary for nursing mothers.

‡ MENOPAUSE

If you are getting hot flashes, it could mean one of two things: either the paparazzi are following you, or you're going through menopause. We have no remedy for the paparazzi, but we can report on two recommendations that have been known to relieve some of the menopausal chaos.

Step into a tub that has 6 inches of cold water in it. Carefully, walk back and forth for about 4 minutes. Be sure to have nonslip stick-ons on the floor of the tub. Step out, dry the feet thoroughly and put on a pair of walking shoes (socks are optional), and take a walk—even if it's just around your room for another 4 minutes.

Naturalists call pure licorice and sarsaparilla, "hormone foods." Use the two of them as teas and drink them often (see "Sources").

‡ CYSTITIS

Women who frequently get cystitis may lessen the number of attacks or stop it forever by passing water immediately after intercourse.

We've heard folk remedies requiring the cystitis sufferer to take baths. Recently, we were told by a research scientist that baths may cause the recurrence of the condition. If you are a bath-taker and have recurring cystitis, refrain from taking a bath for at least a month, and shower instead. You just may find you aren't troubled with cystitis anymore.

According to the American Indians, corn silk (the silky strands beneath the husk of corn), is a cure-all for urinary problems. The most desirable corn silk is from young corns, gathered before the silk turns brown. Take a handful of corn silk and steep it in 3 cups of boiled water for 5 minutes. Strain and drink the 3 cups throughout the day. Corn silk can be stored in a glass jar, not refrigerated. If you can't get corn silk, use corn silk extract, available at most health food stores. Add 10 to 15 drops of the extract to a cup of hot water. *Dried* cornsilk is also available (see "Sources").

‡ BLADDER CONTROL

The Kegel or pubococcygeus exercises can help you gain control over your bladder, strengthen your abdominal muscles and tighten muscles that can enhance sexual activity.

Each time you urinate, start and stop as many times as possible. While squeezing the muscle that stops the flow of urine, pull in on the muscles of the abdomen. You can also do this exercise when *not* urinating. Sit at your desk, in your car, at the movies, anyplace and flex, release, flex, release.

‡ POSTHYSTERECTOMY CARE

After a hysterectomy, drink 2 to 3 cups of pure licorice tea every day and a cup of sarsaparilla tea, too. They are said to help build up the endocrine glands (see "Sources").

‡Gallbladder

The gallbladder is the liver's companion and assistant. Its job is to store bile produced by the liver, then release it to dissolve fats. Your job is to keep the gallbladder healthy and functioning. These remedies may help.

The most popular folk remedy for the gallbladder is black radish. Juice the radish either with a juice extractor or by grating the radish and squeezing it through cheesecloth. Take 1 to 2 tablespoonsful of black radish juice before each meal. Do it for 2 weeks or more. Your digestion should improve and so should the condition of your gallbladder.

An inflamed, irritated or clogged gallbladder can make you feel sluggish and tired, even when you first wake

up in the morning. Take 3 tablespoonsful of fresh lemon juice in half a glass of warm water, a half hour before breakfast. Try this for 1 week and see if there's a difference in your morning energy level. Lemon juice is known to stimulate and cleanse the gallbladder.

If you have had gallbladder surgery, you may help the healing process along with peppermint tea—1 cup 1 hour after eating the 2 biggest meals of the day. Menthol, the active ingredient in peppermint, gives the liver and gallbladder a workout by stimulating bile secretion.

‡Hair

Human hair is almost impossible to destroy. Other than its vulnerability to fire, it cannot be destroyed by changes of climate, water or other natural forces. When you think of the ways some of us abuse our hair with bleaches, dyes, rubber bands, permanents, mousses, sprays and that greasy kid stuff, you can see how resistant it is to all kinds of corrosive chemicals. No wonder it's always clogging up sinks and drainpipes.

While hair may not be *destroyed* by the abuse mentioned above, it may look lifeless and become unmanageable and unhealthy.

One way to tell whether or not hair is healthy is by its stretchability. A strand of adult hair should be able to stretch to 25 percent of its length without breaking. If it's less elastic than that, it's less than healthy.

Here are remedies to help you have healthy hair and be the best tressed person around.

‡ SHAMPOO/TREATMENT FOR CORRECTING AND PREVENTING PROBLEMS

This treatment is said to clean, condition and give a shine to the hair. It should also help get rid of dandruff and nourish the scalp and hair. If it does only half of what it promises, it's worth doing. All you need is:

1 egg yolk and ½ cup warm water for thin and short hair
2 egg yolks and 1 cup warm water for average hair
3 egg yolks and 1½ cups warm water for thick and long hair

Beat the egg yolk(s) and water thoroughly. Massage the mixture into your scalp and on every strand of hair. To make sure the entire head of hair is saturated and fed this protein potion, massage for 5 minutes, then put a plastic bag over your scalp and hair for another 5 minutes. Next, rinse with tepid water (hot water will cook the egg, making it difficult to remove). When you're sure that all of the egg is out of your hair, rinse one more time.

Use this as a maintenance shampoo once or twice a month to help prevent problems from returning.

‡ CONDITIONER FOR WISPY HAIR
This conditioning treatment comes highly recommended for taming flyaway hair. (If you don't know

what we mean, you don't have it.) Beat an egg into 2 ounces (6 tablespoons) of plain yogurt. After shampooing your hair, vigorously rub this mixture into the scalp and hair for 3 minutes. Wrap a towel around your hair and leave it that way for 10 minutes. Rinse with tepid water. If this treatment works for your hair, repeat the procedure after every shampooing.

‡ DRY SHAMPOO

If your building is having plumbing problems, or your city is having a water shortage, or you just don't feel like washing your hair, you can dry shampoo it with cornmeal or cornstarch. Sprinkle some on your hair. Put a piece of cheesecloth or already-run panty hose on the bristles of a hair brush and brush your hair. The cornmeal/cornstarch will pull out the dust from your hair; the cloth will absorb the grease.

Complete the job with a silk scarf. Shine your hair with it, using it as you would a buffing cloth on shoes. After a few minutes of this, if your hair doesn't look clean and shiny, tie the scarf around your head and no one will know the difference.

Coarse or kosher salt is known to be an effective dry shampoo. Put 1 tablespoonful of the salt in silver foil and in the oven to warm for 5 minutes. Using your fingers, work the salt into the scalp and throughout the hair. As soon as you feel that the salt has had a chance to absorb the grease and dislodge the dust, patiently brush it out of your hair. Wash the brush thoroughly, or use an already-clean brush and brush again to make sure all the salt has been removed.

NOTE: Do not use table salt. Not only will you still have dirty hair, but it will look as though you have dandruff, too.

‡ SETTING LOTIONS

Don't throw away beer that's gone flat. Instead, dip your comb in it, comb it through your hair and you have a wonderful setting lotion. Incidentally, the smell of beer seems to disappear quickly.

A friend of ours is a professional model and she knows many tricks of her trade. Her favorite hair-setting lotion is fresh lemon juice. The hair takes longer to dry with the juice on it, but the setting stays in a lot longer. When she runs out of lemons, she uses the bottled lemon juice in the fridge and that works well, too.

If beer or lemon aren't your cup of tea, try milk. Dissolve 4 tablespoonsful of skim milk powder in 1 cup of tepid water. Use it as you would any commercial hair-setting lotion. Unlike most commercial products, the milk helps nourish the scalp and hair.

‡ DANDRUFF

Massage 4 tablespoonsful of warm corn oil into your scalp. Wrap a warm, wet towel around your head and leave it there on the corn oil for half an hour. Shampoo and rinse. Repeat this treatment once a week.

This treatment is for dandruff and other scalp problems. Grate a piece of ginger root and squeeze it through cheesecloth, collecting the juice. Then, mix the ginger juice with an equal amount of sesame oil. Rub the ginger/sesame lotion on the entire scalp, cover the head with a sleep cap or wrap a dish towel around the head and sleep with it on. In the morning, wash with an herbal shampoo (available at most stores where shampoo is sold), and the final rinse should be with 1 tablespoonful of apple cider vinegar in 1 quart of warm water. Repeat this treatment 3 or 4 times a week until the dandruff or other scalp problems vanish.

Prepare chive tea by adding 1 tablespoon of fresh chives to 1 cup of just-boiled water. Cover and let it steep for 20 minutes. Strain and, making sure it's cool, rinse your hair with it right after you shampoo.

You may also want to consider using "Shampoo/ Treatment for Correcting and Preventing Problems"— the first remedy in this chapter.

‡ ENERGIZING HAIR ROOTS

According to reflexology expert Mildred Carter, "To energize the hair roots, grab handsful of hair and yank gently. Do this over the whole head. This is also said to help a hangover, indigestion and other complaints. To further stimulate these reflexes in the head, lightly close your hands into loose fists. With a loose wrist action, lightly pound the whole head. This will not only stimulate the hair, but also the brain, bladder, liver and other organs."

The reflexologist believes that tapping the reflexes in the head with a wire brush can add even greater electrical stimulation to the hair as well as other parts of the body.

‡ STOPPING HAIR LOSS AND PROMOTING HAIR GROWTH

In an average lifetime, the hair on the head grows about 25 feet.

Each of us loses about 100 hairs a day from our scalp. Mostly, the hairs grow back. When they don't, the hairstyle changes from "parted" or "unparted," to "departed."

Ninety percent of baldness can be attributed to hereditary factors. Can something be done to prevent it or overcome it? The people who gave us these remedies say, "Yes!"

An Oriental remedy to stop excessive amounts of hair from falling out is sesame oil. Rub it on your scalp every night. Cover your head with a sleep cap, or wrap it around with a dish towel. In the morning, wash with an herbal shampoo (available at most stores where shampoo is sold). Your final rinse should be with 1 tablespoonful of apple cider vinegar in 1 quart of warm water.

Another version of the above nightly/daily treatment calls for equal amounts of olive oil and oil of rosemary. Combine the two in a bottle and shake vigorously. Then,

rub in scalp, cover the head, sleep, awaken, shampoo and rinse, same as above.

Yet another version of the above nightly/daily procedure—garlic oil. Puncture a couple of garlic perles, squish out all the oil and massage it into your scalp. Then follow the aforementioned routine of covering the head overnight and, in the morning, be sure to shampoo and rinse.

And still another version of these rub-in-scalp remedies: Take half of a raw onion and massage the scalp with it. It's known to be an effective stimulant. Cover the head overnight and shampoo and rinse in the morning.

Just this one more hair-restoring/baldness-preventing formula. A man who recently immigrated to the U.S. from Russia told us that many barbers in the Soviet Union recommend this to their customers. Combine 1 tablespoonful of honey with 1 jigger of vodka and the juice from a medium-size onion. Rub the mixture into the scalp every night, cover, sleep, awaken, shampoo and rinse, as described in the first of this series of remedies.

This was in our first folk remedy book. It's so easy to do, we felt it bears repeating. Three times a day, 5 minutes each time, buff your fingernails with your fingernails. Huh? In other words, rub the fingernails of your right hand across the fingernails of your left hand. Not only is it supposed to stop hair loss, it's also supposed to encourage hair growth and prevent hair from graying.

We heard that Rodney Dangerfield came up with a formula: alum and persimmon juice. It doesn't grow hair. It shrinks your head to fit what hair you've got.

We have one last thought on this obsessive subject of hair loss. There are so many worse things than hair falling out. Think of it this way . . . what if it ached and you had to have it pulled?

‡ "NATURAL" HAIR COLORING
Herbal or vegetable dyes take time because the color must accumulate. Look at this way, if you get the gray out gradually, no one will realize you ever had any gray to begin with.

‡ Brunettes
We have 2 hair-darkening formulas, both with dried sage, which adds life to hair and prevents dandruff.

Prepare dark sage tea by adding 4 tablespoonful of dried sage to 2 cups of just-boiled water and letting it steep for 2 hours. Strain. This dark tea alone will darken gray hair, but for a stronger hair color, add 2 cups of bay rum and 2 tablespoonful of glycerine (available at pharmacies). Bottle this mixture and don't forget to label it. Every night, apply the potion to your hair, starting at the roots and working your way down. Stop the applications when your hair is as dark as you want it to be.

Or, if you're a teetotaler and don't want to use the rum, combine 2 tablespoonful of dried sage with 2 tablespoonful of black tea and simmer in 1 quart of water for 20 minutes. Let it steep for 4 hours, then strain and bottle. Massage it into your hair daily until your hair is the color of your choice. When you need a touch-up, mix a fresh batch of the teas.

Taking sesame seed tea internally has been known to darken one's hair. Crush 2 teaspoonsful of the sesame seeds and bring to a boil in 1 cup of water. Then let it simmer for 20 minutes. As soon as it's cool enough to drink, drink it, seeds and all. Have 2 to 3 cups daily and keep checking the mirror for darkening hair.

Add a little life to your hair color right after you shampoo by pouring a cool cup of espresso through your hair. Let it stay there for 5 minutes and rinse.

‡ **Blondes**
Dried camomile can help add golden highlights to wishy-washy blonde hair. Add 4 tablespoonsful of dried camomile to 2 cups of just-boiled water and let it steep for 2 hours. Strain and use it as a rinse. Be sure to have a basin set up so you can catch the camomile and use it over again after the next 2 or 3 shampoos.

As with most herbal rinses, you mustn't expect dramatic results overnight, if ever. Camomile tea, no matter how strong you make it, will not cover black roots.

That reminds us of something we've wondered about for a while. In Sweden, are there brunettes with blonde roots?

Squeeze the juice out of 2 big lemons, strain and dilute with 1 cup of warm water. Comb the juice through your hair. Be very careful not to get any of it on your skin. Why? Because you should sit in the sun for 15 minutes in order to give your hair the glow of a summer day. If your skin has lemon juice on it, it can cause a burn and give your skin mottled stains.

After the sunbath, rinse your hair thoroughly with warm water, or better yet, with camomile tea.

NOTE: Be sure your skin is properly protected in the sun. See "Sunburn Prevention" in the chapter on "Burns."

‡ **Redheads**

Add radiance to your red hair right after you shampoo by pouring a cup of strong Red Zinger tea (available at health food stores) through your hair. Let it remain there for 5 minutes and rinse.

Juice a raw beet (in a juice extractor) and add 3 times the amount of water as there is juice. Use this as a rinse after shampooing.

NOTE: Since there are many shades of red, we suggest you do a test patch with the beet juice to see how it reacts on your special color.

‡ **Gray, Gray, Go Away!**

Many vitamin therapists have seen proof positive that taking PABA (para-aminobenzoic acid)—300 mg a day—

plus a good B-complex vitamin, also daily, can help change hair back to its original color over a period of 2 months or more.

We got this suggestion from a nutritionist who doesn't have one gray hair in his head. (Of course, he's only twelve years old.)

In a glass of water, mix 2 tablespoonsful of each of the following: apple cider vinegar, raw unheated honey, and blackstrap molasses. Drink this mixture first thing in the morning. Not only should it help you get rid of gray hair, but it should also give you a lot more energy than people who haven't gotten gray yet.

‡ POTPOURRI OF HELPFUL HAIR HINTS

‡ Prevent Gray from Yellowing
By adding a couple of teaspoonsful of laundry bluing to a quart of warm water and using it as your final rinse after shampooing, you can prevent gray hair from turning that yucky yellow.

‡ Green-Hair-From-Pool Treatment
Chlorinated pool water can turn a bleached blonde into the not-so-jolly "green" giant. Dissolve 6 aspirins in a pint of warm water, massage it into your wet hair and the green will never be seen. Rinse thoroughly with clear water. Ho! Ho! Ho!

‡ No-No Number 1: Rubber Bands
We've always been told not to wear rubber bands in our hair. We just found an explanation for it: The rubber insulates the hair and stops the normal flow of static

electricity, so hair elasticity is reduced and the hair breaks more easily.

‡ No-No Number 2: Combing Wet Hair

Combing wet hair stretches it out, causing it to be less elastic and break more easily.

‡ Attention Parents: Gum Remover

To remove gum from hair without doing a Delilah, take a glob of peanut butter, put it on the gummed area, then rub the gum and peanut butter between your fingers until the gum is on its way out. Use a comb to finish the job, then get that careless kid under the faucet for a good shampooing.

‡ A Permanent's Pungent Odor Remover

The distinctive smell of a permanent has a habit of lingering. Tomato juice to the rescue! Saturate your dry hair with tomato juice. Cover your hair and scalp with a plastic bag and stay that way for 10 minutes. Rinse hair thoroughly, then shampoo and rinse again.

‡ Hair Spray Remover

In the middle of shampooing, massage 1 tablespoonful of baking soda into your soaped-up hair. Rinse thoroughly. The baking soda should remove all the hair spray buildup.

‡ Improvised Setting Rollers

If you have long hair and want to experiment setting it with big rollers, try used frozen juice cans, opened at both ends.

‡ Grounding Your Hair

When static electricity makes your hair temporarily unmanageable, you might want to zap it with static spray used on records.

Or, rub a sheet of fabric softener on your hair as well as on your brush or comb.

For chronic wispy hair condition, see "Conditioner for Wispy Hair" earlier in this chapter.

‡Hangovers

Have a hangover? Feel like pulling your hair out? Good idea, but don't go all the way. Just pull your hair, clump by clump, until it hurts a little. According to a noted reflexologist, hair-pulling is stimulating to the entire body and can help lessen the symptoms of a hangover.

When you have a hangover headache, eat a raw persimmon for relief. From now on, if you insist on drinking, make sure it's persimmon season.

Hangover sufferers are often advised to "sleep it off." That's smart advice, since a contributing factor to hangovers is the lack of REM (rapid eye movement) sleep which alcohol seems to suppress. So, yes, sleep it off!

Hungarian Gypsies recommend a bowl of chicken soup with rice. What could be bad?

A glass of sauerkraut juice is said to be effective. If the pure juice is hard for you to take, add some tomato juice to it. Or, eat lots of raw cabbage. That's been known to work wonders.

If you've overindulged and are anticipating waking up in the morning with a hangover, take a vitamin B-complex with 2 or 3 glasses of water before you go to bed. If you pass out before remembering to take the B-complex, when you awaken with your hangover take the vitamin as soon as possible.

Some of the B-complex vitamins are B-1 (thiamine),

B-2 (riboflavin), nicotinamide and pyridoxine. They are helpful in aiding: carbohydrate metabolizing, nerve functioning, the cellular oxidation process and the dilation of blood vessels, all helpful for hangovers. Impressed?

We were on a radio show in Boston and an Irishman called in, identifying himself that way, to share his hangover remedy—the only one that works for him every time: bagel, cream cheese and lox (smoked salmon). He discovered this sure-cure after marrying a Jewish woman who served him the sandwich one morning-after-the-night-before, as a typical Sunday brunch.

There are some of you who will not be happy until you find a "hair of the dog" hangover remedy. Here's one we were told comes from a voodoo practitioner in New Orleans: in a blender, add 1 ounce of Pernod, 1 ounce of white crème de cacao and 3 ounces of milk, plus 3 ice cubes. Blend, drink and good luck!

‡ SOBERING UP

This is a Siberian method of sobering up a tippler. Have him lay flat on his back. Place the palms of your hands on his ears. Next, rub both ears briskly and strongly in a circular motion. Within minutes, the person should start coming around. While he may be a lot more sober than before you rubbed his ears, he should not be trusted behind the wheel of a car.

FACT: For every ounce of alcohol you drink, it takes an hour to regain full driving faculties. In other words, if you have 4 ounces of alcohol by 8 P.M., you should not drive until at least midnight. Actually, we don't think it's a good idea to drive at all on the same night you've done any drinking. Statistics can bear that out.

‡ INTOXICATION PREVENTION

We're reporting the remedies that supposedly prevent one from getting drunk, but we ask that you please take full responsibility for your drinking. If you drink, do not trust or test your reflexes—especially behind the wheel of a car—no matter how sober you seem to feel, or which preventive remedies you take.

American Indians recommend 6 raw (not roasted) almonds before filling up on "fire water."

This remedy comes from healers in West Africa. They suggest eating peanut butter before imbibing. (I wonder if Annette Funicello knows this.)

Gem therapists tell of the power of amethysts. In Greek, "amethyst" is "ametusios" and means "remedy against drunkenness." Please don't take this to mean that if you carry an amethyst and you drink, you won't get drunk. It's that carrying an amethyst should give one the strength to refuse a drink and, *therefore*, prevent intoxication.

‡ WOMEN, TAKE HEED

Women who drink right before menstruating, when their estrogen level is low, get drunk more easily and usually become more nauseated with rougher hangovers than during the rest of their cycle.

‡ EASING THE URGE FOR ALCOHOL

According to medical researcher Carlson Wade, a tangy beverage can ease and erase the urge to imbibe. He recommends a glass of tomato juice with the juice of 1 lemon added and you might also want to throw in a couple of ice cubes. Stir well. Sip as slowly as you would an alcoholic drink.

‡Headaches

We said this in our first folk remedy book and it bears repeating. Take a holistic approach to yourself and your headache. Step back and look at the past 24 hours of your life. Have you eaten sensibly? Did you get a decent night's sleep? Have you moved your bowels since awakening this morning? Are there deadlines you need to meet? Do you have added pressures at home or at work? Is there something you're dreading?

Since studies show that more than 90 percent of headaches are brought on by nervous tension, most of our remedies are for the common tension headache and a few for the more serious migraines.

In the case of regularly recurring headaches, they can be caused by eyestrain, or something as seemingly silly as gum chewing, or a lack of negative ions in the air, or an allergy, or something more serious. We suggest you consult with a health professional to determine the cause of recurring headaches.

Headaches are a headache! Use your instincts, common sense and patience to find what works best for you and your headache.

Research scientists tell us that almonds contain salicylates, the pain-relieving ingredient in aspirin. Eat 15 raw almonds to do the work of 1 aspirin. While it may take a little longer for the headache to vanish, you don't run the risk of side effects. (What the scientists need to find now are fast-acting almonds.)

Get a little bottle of essence of rosemary and rub a small amount of the oil on your forehead and temples, also behind your ears. Then inhale the fumes from the open bottle 4 times. If your headache doesn't disappear within half an hour, repeat the rubbing and inhaling once more.

This seems to be a favorite of some Indian gurus: Add 1 teaspoonful of dried basil to 1 cup of hot water, let it cook, then add 2 tablespoonsful of witch hazel. Saturate a washcloth with the mixture and apply it to the forehead. Bandage it in place and keep it there until the washcloth dries or your headache disappears, whichever comes first.

This will either work for you, or it won't. You'll find out quickly and easily. Dunk your hands into water that's as hot as you can stand without scalding yourself. Keep them there for 1 minute. If you don't start feeling relief within 15 minutes, go on to another remedy.

If your tension headache seems to stem from the tightness in your neck, use an electric heating pad or a very warm, wet cloth around your neck. The heat should relax you and improve circulation.

If you like to garden and grow your own herbs including mint, take a large mint leaf, bruise it, then roll it up and stick it in your nostril. It is *not* a pretty picture.

A Mexican folk remedy says to paste a fresh mint leaf on the part of the head where the pain is most severe.

In England, the mint leaf is juiced and the juice is used as eardrops to relieve a headache.

Grate a potato (a red one if possible), or an apple, and make a poultice out of it. Apply the poultice to your forehead and bandage it in place, keeping it there for at least an hour.

You might want to try some acupressure to get rid of that headache. Stick out your tongue about ½ an inch and bite down on it as hard as you can without hurting yourself. Stay that way for *exactly 10 minutes*, not a minute more!

Some people rid themselves of headache pain by taking vitamin C—500 mg every hour—to dilate the constricted blood vessels that are thought to cause the pain. If, after a few hours, you still have a headache, this isn't working for you. Stop taking vitamin C and try another remedy.

The fact that you have this book leads us to believe that you're a person who's interested in and open to all kinds of alternatives, variety and new adventures. (If you're a single man and over forty, will you marry me? And do you have a single brother? But seriously . . .) Usually, when a person is adventurous, it extends to his/her eating habits. And so we would like to introduce you to daikon, a Japanese radish (if you aren't already familiar with it). It's delicious eaten raw in salads and wonderful for digestion, especially when eating oily foods.

Meanwhile, back to the headache remedy. Grate a piece of daikon and squeeze out the juice through cheesecloth on to a washcloth. Apply the washcloth to your forehead and bandage in place. It should help draw out the pain.

While we're talking "exotic edibles," as remedies (see above), you should know about gomasio—that's Japanese for sesame salt. You can buy it at health food stores. The interesting thing about this seasoning is that the oil from the crushed sesame seeds coats the sea salt so that it doesn't cause an excessive attraction for water. In other words, you can season food with it and it won't make you thirsty the way regular salt does.

To get relief from a headache, eat (thoroughly chew) 1 teaspoonful of gomasio.

Add ½ teaspoonful of angelica (see "Sources") to ¾ cup of hot water and drink. It not only helps ease the pain of a headache, but it is said to give a person a lighter happier feeling.

Niacin has helped many headache sufferers when all else has failed (see "Migraine Headaches"—the first remedy).

‡ MIGRAINE HEADACHES

Niacin, when taken at the first sign of a migraine, has been known to prevent it from getting to be a full-blown, torturous headache. To prevent or get rid of a headache, take anywhere from 50 to 100 mg at a time. The higher the dosage, the stronger the side effects. For most people, the side effects are felt when they take 100 mg and up. Both of us get the "niacin flush" that makes us look like we've been in the sun too long. It's usually accompanied by itching and/or tingling. It lasts about 15 minutes and is not at all harmful. Niacinamide is said to be as effective as niacin, but without the side effects.

Bathe your feet in a basin of very strong, hot black coffee. Some medical professionals recommend drinking a cup or 2 of coffee as well. Or, for the same effectiveness, but less caffeine, drink yerba maté, also called Paraguay tea (see "Sources").

Ready for this one? Sit under a hair dryer. The heat and high-pitched hum may relax the tension that brought on the headache. According to Dr. Robert B. Taylor, our source for this remedy, the dryer brings relief to two thirds of the migraine sufferers who try it. Your local beautician will probably be happy to accommodate you if you promise not to get a headache during their busy time.

Buy a bunch of beets with leaves and follow these directions. Scrub a beet and wash and bruise the leaves. Grate a piece of the beet and squeeze out the juice through cheesecloth, enough juice to fill an eyedropper. Cut about 5 silver-dollar-size slices of the beet and eat them. Take the leaves and put them on your forehead, binding them in place with a bandage. Now fill the eyedropper with the beet juice, lie down and put half the dropperful in one nostril, the other half in the other nostril. Lie quietly (you need a rest after all of that) for half an hour. Hopefully, within that time, your migraine will start to subside.

Open a jar of strong mustard and slowly inhale the fumes several times. This has been known to help ease the pain for some people.

Some people have migraines without having severe headaches. Instead, they are troubled by impaired vision—spots in front of their eyes or seeing double. We heard about a simple remedy. Chew a handful of raisins. Chew them thoroughly before swallowing.

You never know which remedy is going to work best until you try it. Have you tried squatting in 8 inches of hot water (in your bathtub, of course) for 20 minutes?

‡ HEADACHE PREVENTION . . . SORT OF

A 3-year study at the University of Michigan showed that students who ate 2 apples a day had far fewer headaches than those who didn't eat any apples. The apple eaters also had fewer skin problems, arthritic conditions and colds.

You might want to have an apple for breakfast and 1 as a late afternoon snack, or 1 a couple of hours after dinner. Those are the best times to eat fruit.

Chances are, eating 2 apples a day will also prevent constipation, which is a leading cause of headaches.

‡Heart

‡ HEART ATTACK

If you or someone you're with feels as though they're having a heart attack, call for professional medical help immediately. While you're waiting for help to arrive, squeeze the end of the little finger on the left hand. Squeeze it HARD! Keep squeezing it. This acupressure procedure has been said to save lives.

Like the above remedy, this one has also been known to save lives while waiting for professional help to arrive when someone is having a heart attack. Dr. John R. Christopher, master herbalist, says to put 1 teaspoonful of cayenne pepper in a glass of warm water and have the patient force himself to drink it all. Cayenne pepper is hotter than hot and hard to take, but so is having a heart attack.

‡ HEART HELPERS

According to the results of a study, orchestra conductors live an average of 7½ years longer than the average person.

To strengthen your heart, tone up your circulatory system and have some fun, go through the motions of conducting an orchestra. Do it for at least 10 minutes a day, or 20 minutes 3 days a week. Conduct to music that inspires you. If you don't have a baton, use a ruler or a chopstick. Pretend each day of exercise is a command performance. Throw your whole self into it physically and emotionally.

NOTE: If you have a history of heart problems, be sure to check with your doctor before you begin your new career as a make-believe conductor.

Two teaspoonsful of raw honey a day, either in a glass of water, or straight off the spoon, is thought by many nutritionists to be the best tonic for strengthening the heart, as well as for general physical repair.

Someone just told us: "Once you reach the age of 40, it's repair, repair, repair."

Okay, so you don't want to join a gym. You don't have to. For the best exercise and the perfect body stimulator, just take an old-fashioned walk—make it a brisk old-fashioned walk—daily.

Incidentally, walking is believed to use the same amount of energy as running.

According to Dr. Richard Passwater, vitamin B-15 quickens the healing of scar tissue around the heart and also limits the side effects of some heart medication. The suggested dosage is 150 mg a day along with a B-complex vitamin.

This remedy is recommended for people who have a history of heart problems. Right before going to bed, take a 10-minute foot bath. Step into calf-high water, as hot as you can take it without scalding yourself. As the minutes pass and the water cools, add more hot water. After 10 minutes, step out of the tub and dry your feet thoroughly, preferably with a rough towel. Once your feet are dry, give them a 1-minute massage, manipulating the toes as well as the entire foot. This foot bath/massage may help circulation, remove congestion around the heart and pave the way to a peaceful night's sleep.

We recently read a list of supposed benefits of hawthorn berries. We followed up by researching the herb and as a result, we now take 2 capsules—565 mg each— after every meal.

Included on that list of benefits were: normalizes blood pressure by regulating heart action; improves heart valve defects; helps people with a lot of stress; strengthens weakened heart muscle, and prevents arteriosclerosis (hardening of the arteries).

‡ ARTERIOSCLEROSIS (HARDENING OF THE ARTERIES)

You might want to check out the remedies in "Heart Helpers," particularly the last one about hawthorn berries.

Garlic is suggested for just about every ailment, either in our first folk remedy book or this one, so why not for arteriosclerosis too? A couple of cloves of garlic a day has been known to unplug arteries. It seems to really do a job cleansing the system, collecting and casting out toxic waste. Mince the 2 cloves and put them in ½ glass of orange juice or water and drink it down. There's no need to chew the pieces of garlic. By just swallowing them, the garlic smell doesn't stay on your breath.

In conjunction with a sensible diet, garlic can also help bring down cholesterol levels in the blood. No wonder this beautiful bulb has a fan club, appropriately called, "Lovers of the Stinking Rose." (Interested in joining? See "Sources.")

Rutin is one of the elements of the bioflavonoids. Bioflavonoids are necessary for the proper absorption of vitamin C. Taking 500 mg of rutin daily, with at least the same amount of vitamin C, is said to increase the strength of capillaries, strengthen the artery walls, help prevent hemorrhaging and help treat arteriosclerosis.

‡ CHOLESTEROL

After researching the subject of cholesterol, our understanding is that there's a harmful cholesterol component (LDL) and a protective cholesterol component (HDL).

Test results we've heard about are very impressive and build a good case for the effectiveness of lecithin lowering LDL levels and raising HDL levels.

DOSE: 1-2 tablespoonsful of lecithin granules daily.

The American Journal of Clinical Nutrition mentioned that raw carrots not only improve elimination because of their high fiber content, but may also lower cholesterol. Test subjects who ate 2 carrots for breakfast for 3 weeks reduced their serum cholesterol level by 11 percent.

You might want to scrub the carrots you eat instead of peeling them. The peel is rich in B-1 (thiamin), B-2 (riboflavin), and B-3 (niacin).

We said it before, we'll say it again: Alfalfa sprouts! Buy them or grow them yourself and eat them every day. It is said that alfalfa can lower cholesterol levels in one's system. (For more on sprouts, see: "Preparation Guide.")

It seems that very small amounts of chromium are vital for good health. A deficiency in chromium may be linked to coronary artery disease. Take 1-2 tablespoonsful of brewer's yeast daily (be sure to read labels and select the brewer's yeast with the highest chromium content), or a handful of raw sunflower seeds. The chromium, like the lecithin, is said to lower the LDL cholesterol level and raise the HDL cholesterol level. If you plan on doing this, consult with your doctor first.

Oats can bring down blood cholesterol levels, Dr. Hans Fischer, nutritionist at Rutgers University, concluded after studying results done with test groups. One can reap this benefit by eating oatmeal or any other form of oats 2 or 3 times a week.

This remedy comes from a very recent report. The report falls into the you-can-go-crazy-with-all-of-this category.

Dr. Scott Grundy, professor at the University of Texas Health Science Center in Dallas, says that the new findings show that *mono*unsaturated fatty acid found in olive oil and peanut oil is more effective in reducing artery-clogging cholesterol levels of blood than *poly*unsaturated fats such as corn oil and sunflower oil.

The truth, can't you go crazy with all of this?

‡ PALPITATIONS

If you have palpitations (and who hasn't at one time or another), take a holistic approach to find the cause. Was it the MSG in the Chinese food you had for lunch? Or the caffeine in the chocolate you pigged out on? Pressure at the office? Cigarette smoke? Sugar? Work at figuring it out so that you learn what not to have next time.

Meanwhile, here's a natural sedative to subdue the thumping. Steep 2 camomile tea bags in 2 cups of just-boiled water. Steam a few shredded leaves of cabbage. Then, in a soup bowl, combine the steamed leaves with the camomile tea. This tea-soup may not taste good, but it can help overcome those skipped heartbeats.

‡Hemorrhoids

Put the tobacco from 2 cigarettes in a pan, add 4 teaspoonsful of butter and let the mixture simmer for a couple of minutes. Next, pour the hot liquid through a strainer onto a sanitary napkin. When it's cool enough, apply it to the hemorrhoid area. Whip up a fresh batch 3 times a day.

WARNING: Once you start doing this, you may not want to stop. Well, don't they say tobacco is habit-forming?

A consulting doctor for the Denver Broncos and Denver Nuggets has had success in speeding up athlete's hemorrhoid healing processes with vitamin C baths. The doctor recommends 1 cup of ascorbic acid powder to every 5 quarts of cool bath water. Sit in the tub for 15 minutes at a time, 2 or 3 times a day. Ascorbic acid powder is expensive. If you can fit your tushy into a basin with ½ cup of the powder and 2½ quarts of cool water, you'll save a fortune.

Take advantage of the healing properties of papaya by drenching a wad of sterilized cotton in pure papaya juice. Position it on the hemorrhoid area and secure it in place. The juice should help stop the bleeding and bring the irritation under control.

‡Herpes (All Kinds— Genitalis, Simplex, Etc.)

Twenty million Americans (1 out of every 5 sexually active adults) have herpes. Each year 300,000 to 500,000 more get it.

We spoke with a man who did extensive research and came up with a remedy for overcoming the symptoms (fever blisters, cold sores, etc.) of herpes. He tested it and had friends test it. The results were impressive. But first, the remedy, next the explanation, and then, more about the results.

Do not eat nuts, chocolate or (sorry Mom) chicken soup. At the first sign of a herpes flare-up, eat 1 pound of steamed flounder. That's it. That's the remedy.

The explanation in simple terms, as best as we understood it, is that there's a certain ratio in the body of 2 amino acids—arginine and lysine. To contract herpes and to have the symptoms recur, one's body has to have a high level of arginine compared to the level of lysine. The secret then, is to reduce the amount of arginine (eliminate nuts, chocolate and chicken soup), and increase the amount of lysine (eat flounder). The pound of flounder has 11,000 mg of lysine. You can take lysine tablets, but you would have to take so many of them, and besides, they have binders and other things you just don't need. Also, the tablets are not as digestible or as absorbable as the lysine in flounder. By steaming the fish, you keep most of the nutrients in it. You can add the sauce of your choice to the flounder once it's been steamed.

As for results, the man and his friends have had symptoms disappear overnight after eating flounder and *never* eating nuts, chocolate and (oh, how we hate to say it) chicken soup.

‡Hiccups

Locate the area about 2 to 3 inches above your navel and between the two sides of your rib cage. Press in with the fingers of both of your hands and hold there long enough to say to yourself: one, two, three, four, I don't have the hiccups anymore. If you still have them, try reciting *The Ancient Mariner*.

Close your eyes, hold your breath and think of 10 bald men. Let us start you off: Telly Savalas.

Pardon our name dropping, but . . . When we were on the *Today Show*, Jane Pauley told us that her husband, Garry Trudeau, gets painful hiccups. His remedy is to put a teaspoonful of salt on half a lemon and then suck the juice out of the lemon.

Our Great Aunt Molly used to soak a cube of sugar in fresh lemon juice and then let it dissolve in her mouth. She did it to get rid of the hiccups. She also did it as a shortcut whenever she drank tea.

Just visualizing a rabbit . . . its cute little face, quivering nose and white whiskers . . . has been known to make the hiccups disappear.

One of the most common remedies for hiccups is a teaspoonful of granulated sugar. It supposedly irritates the throat, causing the interruption of the vagus nerve impulse pattern that is responsible for triggering the spasms of the diaphragm. (Just reading the previous sentence aloud may help you get rid of the hiccups.)

In Arabia, people have been known to use sand in place of sugar. We haven't tried either remedy since we don't eat sugar and we don't go to the beach.

Another way you might interrupt the diaphragmatic spasms is by holding your arms above your head and panting like a dog. Well, you may not get rid of the hiccups, but you may end up with some table scraps.

Lay a broom on the floor and jump over it six times. If you want to update this remedy, try jumping over a vacuum cleaner. For all you rich people, jump over your maid.

Turn yourself into a "t" by spreading out your arms. Then give a big yawn.

Pretend you're chewing gum while your fingers are in your ears, gently pressing inward. "What? I can't hear you. My fingers are in my ears."

‡ WHEN SOMEONE ELSE HAS THE HICCUPS . . .

Take something cold that's made of metal—a spoon is good—tie a string around it and lower it down the hiccupper's back.

Suddenly accuse the hiccupper of doing something (s)he did not do. "You left the water running in the tub!" "You borrowed money from me and forgot to pay it back!"

‡Indigestion

In our great land of plenty, one of the most common ailments is indigestion. We have a friend who always wears a plaid suit so he can keep a check on his stomach. But seriously, folks . . .

Persistent indigestion may be due to a food allergy. You may need a health professional to help you check it out. Severe indigestion may be something a lot more serious than you think. Seek professional help immediately.

CAUTION: Never take a laxative when you have severe stomach pain.

Mild indigestion usually produces one or a combination of the following symptoms: stomachache, nausea and vomiting, gas and/or heartburn.

Relief may be a page or two away.

When you have stomach cramps caused by indigestion, take 1 teaspoonful of apricot brandy as your after-dinner drink.

In the case of acid indigestion, chew dry rolled oats. After chewing a teaspoonful thoroughly, swallow them.

The oats not only soothe the acid condition, they also neutralize it.

We keep daikon in the refrigerator at all times. It's a Japanese radish . . . white, crisp and delicious. It's an effective digestive aid, especially when eating heavy, deep-fried foods. Either grate 1 to 2 tablespoonsful or have a couple of slices of the daikon with your meal. It also helps detoxify animal protein and fats.

When you have a white-coated tongue, bad breath and a headache, it's probably due to an upset stomach. A wise choice of herbs would be sage. Sip a cup of sage tea slowly.

We have come across some strange-sounding remedies for which there seem to be no logical explanation. We've included a few of them, simply because they sometimes work. This is one of them: tie a red string around your stomach when it aches. If the pain disappears, fine. If not, go on to another remedy.

When you have a sour stomach, chew a few anise seeds, cardamom seeds or caraway seeds. They'll sweeten your stomach and your breath as well.

Like rolled oats (one of the previous remedies), raw potato juice also neutralizes acidity. Grate a potato and squeeze it through cheesecloth to get the juice. Dilute 1 tablespoonful of potato juice with ½ cup of warm water. Drink it slowly.

Take a wire hairbrush or a metal comb and brush or comb the backs of your hands for 3 to 4 minutes. It's supposed to relieve that sluggish feeling one gets from eating one of those old-fashioned, home-cooked, the-cholesterol-can-kill-ya' meals.

This was recommended to us for a nervous stomach. Add ¼ teaspoonful of oregano and ½ teaspoonful of marjoram to 1 cup of hot water. Let it steep for 10 minutes. Strain and sip slowly. Two hours later, if you still have stomach uneasiness, drink another cup of the mixture.

This remedy from India is recommended for quick relief after a junk-food binge. Crush 1 teaspoonful of fenugreek seeds and steep them in 1 cup of just-boiled water for 5 minutes. Strain and drink slowly. One should feel better in about 10 minutes.

According to a Chinese massage therapist, if you are having stomach discomfort, there will be tender areas at the sides of your knees, just below the knee caps. As you massage those spots and the tenderness decreases, so should the corresponding stomachache.

‡ INDIGESTION PREVENTION

A Jewish doctor we know practices preventive medicine on himself before eating Szechuan or Mexican food or any other "hot" food that would ordinarily give him an upset stomach. He takes 1 tablespoonful of olive oil about 15 minutes before the meal.

We've heard that 1 teaspoonful of whole white mustard seeds taken before a meal may help prevent stomach distress.

‡ NAUSEA AND VOMITING

When you have an upset stomach and you're feeling nauseous, take a carbonated drink—seltzer, club soda, Perrier or some ginger ale. If you don't have any of those, and you're not on a sodium-restricted diet, mix 1 teaspoonful of baking soda with 1 glass of cold water and drink slowly. Within a few minutes, you should burp and feel better.

Drink 1 cup of yarrow tea (see "Sources"). This herb is known to stop nausea in next to no time. It's also wonderful for helping tone up the digestive system.

When the food you ate seems to be laying on your chest, or you have a bad case of stomach overload, and you know you'd feel much better if you threw up, reach for the English mustard. It's available at food specialty shops. Drink 1 teaspoonful in a glass of warm water. If you don't upchuck in 10 minutes, drink another glass of this mustard water. After another 10 minutes, if it still hasn't worked, the third time should be the charm. I'm getting nauseous just thinking about all the watered-down mustard.

To help ease a severe bout of vomiting, warm ½ cup of vinegar, saturate a washcloth in it and place the moist cloth on your bare stomach with a hot water bottle on top of the cloth.

‡ GAS/FLATULENCE

Are you sure it's gas and not your appendix? To test for appendix problems, in a standing position, lift your right leg and then quickly jut it forward as though kicking something. If you have an excruciating, sharp pain anywhere in the abdominal area, it may be your appendix, in which case, seek medical attention immediately. If there is no sharp pain when you kick, it's probably just gas, but you may want to check with your doctor to be sure.

By now, you probably know which foods give you gas and which meals may prove lethal. But do you know about food combining? The library has lots of books with information on the subject, and there are simple, inexpensive charts sold at health food stores. If you follow proper food combining—for example, wait 2 hours after eating regular food before eating fruit—you shouldn't ever have a problem with gas. It's not always convenient to stick to good combinations. Here are some remedies for when your food combining is less than perfect and as a result, you're cooking with gas.

When you know you're eating food that's going to make you and everyone around you sorry you ate it, take 2 charcoal tablets or capsules as soon as you finish your meal. It's important to take the charcoal quickly because gas forms in the lower intestine and if you wait too long, the charcoal can't get down there fast enough to help.

WARNING: Do not take charcoal capsules or tablets

often. They are a powerful adsorbent and will rob you of the nutrients you need.

Each one of the following seeds is known to give fast relief from the pain of gas: anise seeds, caraway seeds, dill seeds or fennel seeds. To release the essential oils from the seeds, gently crush 1 teaspoonful and add it to a cup of just-boiled water. Let it steep for 10 minutes. Strain and drink. If the gas pains don't disappear right away, drink another cup of the seed tea before eating your next meal.

The unripe berries of a pimento evergreen tree are called allspice. It was given its name because it tastes like a combination of spices: cloves, juniper berries, cinnamon and pepper. Allspice is said to be effective in treating flatulent indigestion. Add 1 teaspoonful of powdered allspice to a cup of just-boiled water and drink. If you have the dried fruit, chew ½ teaspoonful, then swallow.

If you feel you have a gas pocket, or trapped gas, lie down on the floor or on a bed and slowly bring your knees up to your chest to the count of 10, then back down. In between this exercise, massage your stomach in a circular motion, with the top half of your fingers, pressing hard to move that gas around and out.

‡ HEARTBURN
Certain foods may not agree with you, causing a condition known as heartburn. My mother used to get heartburn a lot. I remember asking her, "How do you

know when you have it?" My mother said, "You'll know!" She was right.

Keep chewable papaya tablets with you and at the first sign of heartburn, or any kind of indigestion, pop papaya pills in your mouth, chew and swallow.

A cup of peppermint tea has been known to relieve the discomfort of heartburn.

Eat a teaspoonful of gomasio (sesame seeds and sea salt, available at health food stores).

This may not be too appetizing, but it works: a teaspoonful or 2 of uncooked oat flakes, *well chewed*.

The flow of saliva can neutralize the stomach acids that slosh up and cause heartburn. According to Dr. Wylie Dodds at the Medical College of Wisconsin, chewing gum (we suggest sugarless), can increase the production of saliva 8 or 9 times, and reduce the damage caused by stomach acids.

‡Infants and Children

Every baby-care book tells you to "childproof" your home. Make a crawling tour of each room in your house in order to see things from a child's-eye-view. Once you're aware of the danger zones, you can eliminate them by covering wires, nailing down furniture, etc. Do this every 4 to 6 months as the child grows and is able to reach more things.

Still, no matter how childproof a place is, a mishap can happen. We suggest that parents have a first-aid book handy and/or take a first-aid course through the local American Red Cross.

It's also very important to keep a list of the following emergency numbers near every telephone in the house:

- Pediatrician
- Poison Control Center
- Police
- Fire Department
- Hospital
- Pharmacy
- Dentist
- Neighbors (with cars)

In terms of home remedies for common conditions, we caution you that children's systems are much more delicate than ours. While lots of the remedies throughout the book can certainly be applied to youngsters, use good common sense in prescribing doses and strengths. In all cases, check with the pediatrician first.

One major caution: NEVER GIVE HONEY TO A

CHILD UNDER ONE YEAR OLD! Spores found in honey have been linked to botulism in babies.

Here are some remedies specifically for children's ailments. They should help you as well as your child to get through those tough times.

‡ APPETITE STIMULANT

Prepare a cup of camomile tea and add $\frac{1}{16}$ teaspoonful of ground ginger. An herbalist recommends 1 teaspoonful of the warm tea half an hour before meals to stimulate a child's appetite.

‡ BEDWETTING

This exercise strengthens the muscles that control urination: starting with the first urination of the day, have the child start and stop urinating as many times as possible until (s)he has finished. If you make it into a game, counting the number of starts and stops, the child might look forward to breaking his or her own record each time. It's important, however, not to pressure the child into feeling inadequate if (s)he finds this exercise difficult.

‡ CHICKEN POX

Of course a child with chicken pox should be in bed, kept warm and on a light diet, including lots of pure fruit juices. Yarrow tea, according to herbalists, seems to be the thing for children's eruptive ailments. Add 1 tablespoonful of dried yarrow (see "Sources") to 2 cups of just-boiled water and let it steep for 10 minutes.

Strain, then add 1 tablespoonful of raw honey. Give the child ½ cupful 3 or 4 times a day.

To relieve the itching, a pediatrician recommends a spritz of ordinary spray starch on the itchy areas.

‡ COLDS

The results of a study published by two doctors in a respected scientific journal were that zinc gluconate lozenges can shorten the duration of a cold dramatically. The lozenges (honey-flavored are the best; lemon are the pits) should not be taken on an empty stomach. Even if the child is not eating much because of the cold, have him or her eat half a fruit before sucking a lozenge.

DOSE: If a child weighs less than 60 pounds, (s)he should take 6 zinc lozenges, 23 mg each, per day, not more. For teenagers, the maximum dose is 9 lozenges, 23 mg each, per day.

IMPORTANT: Do not give the child lozenges for more than 2 days in a row.

‡ COLIC

A popular European colic calmer is fennel tea. Add ½ teaspoonful of fennel seeds to 1 cup of just-boiled water and let it steep for 10 minutes. Strain the liquid tea into the baby's bottle. When it's cool enough to drink, give it to the baby. If (s)he's not thrilled with the taste of fennel, try dill seeds instead.

Caraway seeds are said to bring relief to colicky kids (and parents and neighbors). Add 1 tablespoonful of bruised caraway seeds to 1 cup of just-boiled water. Let it steep for 10 minutes. Strain and put 2 teaspoonsful of the tea into the baby's bottle. When it's cool enough to drink, give it to the baby.

If you are breast-feeding your baby and (s)he is colicky, try eliminating milk from *your* diet. There's a 50–50 chance that if you no longer drink milk, the baby will no longer have colic. Be sure, however, to eat calcium-rich foods such as salmon, sardines, sunflower and sesame seeds, whole grains, green leafy vegetables, soybean products, including tofu, and molasses.

‡ COUGH

Add ½ teaspoonful of anise seeds and ½ teaspoonful of thyme to 1 cup of just-boiled water. Let it steep for 10 minutes. Stir it, strain and let cool. Then add a teaspoonful of honey.

DOSE: 1 tablespoonful every half hour. THIS IS FOR CHILDREN ABOVE THE AGE OF TWO YEARS OLD.

A woman from Oklahoma called to tell us that whenever her child gets a cough that acts up at night, she loosely ties a black cotton thread around the child's neck. IT MUST BE BLACK. This woman said she tried other colors and nothing but the black works.

We were intrigued with the remedy and tested it on our friend. It worked like magic. We researched it and sure enough, found a printed source that credited it to shamans in ancient Egypt.

‡ CROUP

Scottish folk healers treat the croup by wrapping a piece of bacon (uncooked, of course) around the child's neck, bundling him up in a blanket and taking him into a steamy bathroom for a few minutes.

It's something to do till the doctor arrives.

‡ DIARRHEA

From the Pennsylvania Dutch comes this children's remedy for diarrhea. In a warmed cup of milk, add $\frac{1}{16}$ teaspoonful of cinnamon. The child should drink as much as possible.

Raspberry leaf tea is excellent for treating diarrhea. Combine $\frac{1}{2}$ ounce of dried raspberry leaves with 1 cup of water and simmer in an enamel or glass saucepan for 25 minutes. Strain and let the liquid cool to room temperature.

DOSE: For a baby under 1 year, $\frac{1}{2}$ teaspoonful 4 times a day; for a child over 1 year, 1 teaspoonful 4 times a day.

‡ DIGESTION

If a baby can't seem to keep his food down, you may want to try putting a teaspoonful of carob powder in the baby's formula. In some instances it may make the difference.

‡ FOREIGN SUBSTANCE IN THE NOSE

Lots of kids stick things up their nose. Lydia put a yankee bean in her nostril when she was three years old, and it began to take root. Luckily, our father noticed that she was sitting still for more than 30 seconds at a time, so he realized something was wrong.

Before you take the child to the doctor to perform a yankee beanectomy, open the child's mouth, place your mouth over it and briskly blow once. Your gust of breath may dislodge the object from the child's nostril. If it doesn't after that first try, seek medical attention.

‡ MEASLES

Yarrow tea is good for eruptive ailments (see "Chicken Pox" earlier). To strengthen the child's eyes, which are usually affected when one has the measles, and to ease the discomfort in them, make sure the child gets food rich in vitamin A—carrot juice, cantaloupe and green and yellow fruit.

‡ PIMPLY-FACED INFANTS

It's common to see infants with an outbreak of pimples. According to a folk remedy from the 1600s, gently dab the premature case of acne with mother's milk. If you're not nursing the baby, use a few drops of whole milk (not skim milk).

‡ PRICKLY HEAT

Gently rub the afflicted area with a watermelon rind.

‡ TONSILITIS

We've been told about lots of cases of swollen tonsils because of an intolerance for milk. That's easy enough to test. Simply eliminate milk from the child's diet and check the results within a day or two. If the child does not assimilate milk properly, there are many other wonderful sources of calcium and it is no big deal for a child not to have milk. Sesame seeds are rich in calcium, so are green leafy vegetables, shellfish, molasses and whole grains. There are also supplements: bone meal, dolomite and calcium lactate. Check with a health professional.

Master herbalist Dr. John R. Christopher says that puberty will be easier to go through if the teenagers still have their tonsils. The girls will have easier menstrual periods and the boys will have less chance for prostate malfunction. The reason is that the tonsils are the filtering system for the reproductive organs and are needed by the body.

‡Kidney and Bladder

Noted psychic healer, Edgar Cayce, said of the almond, "An almond a day is much more in accord with keeping the doctor away than apples." Almonds have nutritious, health-promoting properties. The following almond mixture is especially healing in the treatment of kidney and bladder disorders:

Put ½ cup of blanched almonds in a blender and blend it to a paste. Transfer the almond paste to a glass and slowly stir in barley water (see "Preparation Guide") until the consistency is that of a thick shake. Enjoy this drink once a day for 7 days.

Our gem therapist friend recommends wearing jade against the skin to help heal kidney and bladder problems. If your mate reads this and surprises you with a piece of jade jewelry, chances are you'll start to feel better immediately.

Lots of folk remedies include the use of apple cider vinegar to help flush the kidneys and to provide a natural acid. Dosage varies from source to source. We think it makes most sense to take 1 teaspoonful of apple cider vinegar for every 50 pounds you weigh, and add it to 6 ounces of water. In other words, if you weigh 150 pounds, the dosage would be 3 teaspoonsful of vinegar in 6 ounces of water. Drink it twice a day, before breakfast and before dinner. Keep it up for 2 days, then stop for 4 days. Continue this 2-days-yes/4-days-no cycle as long as you feel you need it.

Aduki (or azuki) beans, found in health food stores, are used in the Orient as food and medicine. They're excellent for treating kidney problems. Rinse a cupful of aduki beans. Combine the cup of beans with 5 cups of water and boil for 1 hour. Strain the aduki-bean water into a jar. Drink ½ cup of aduki water at least ½ hour before meals. Do this for 2 days—6 meals. To prevent the aduki water from spoiling, keep the jar in the refrigerator, then warm the water before drinking.

Incidentally, raw aduki beans are fun to sprout (see: "Preparation Guide"), good to eat and have rejuvenating powers.

‡ INCONTINENCE

This remedy comes from the Hottentot tribe of South Africa where buchu shrubs grow. Steep 1 tablespoonful of buchu leaves (see "Sources") in 1 cup of just-boiled water for half an hour.

DOSE: 3 to 4 tablespoonsful, 3 to 4 times a day. Buchu leaves are known to be helpful for many urinary problems including inflammation of the bladder and painful urination as well as incontinence.

‡ BEDWETTING

Just when you may have thought that nothing could help, heeeeeere's uva ursi! This herb is said to strengthen the urinary tract and, taken in small doses, has been known to end bedwetting.

Add 1 tablespoonful of the dried uva ursi leaves or 1 tea bag to 1 cup of just-boiled water and steep for 5 minutes. Strain into a jar.

DOSE: 1 tablespoonful before each meal every day for 6 weeks. (Uva ursi is available at health food stores or see: "Sources.")

NOTE: Arbutin, the main component of the herb, uva ursi, may cause the urine to turn brownish in color. It's absolutely nothing to worry about.

ANOTHER NOTE: We do not list this as a children's bedwetting remedy because none of our sources mentioned it for children. The herb may be too strong for their small systems.

‡Male Problems

‡ ENLARGED PROSTATE

It is estimated that one out of every three men over the age of 60 has some kind of prostate problem.

We strongly suggest that if you are suffering with pain, burning, testicular or scrotal swelling, or any other prostate-related symptoms, you have your condition evaluated by a health professional.

Grate part of a yellow onion and squeeze it through cheesecloth—enough for a tablespoonful of onion juice. Take 1 tablespoonful of onion juice twice a day.

In extremely painful cases, mix ½ teaspoonful of powdered slippery elm bark (see "Sources") with warm water. Drink the mixture before breakfast and a couple of hours after dinner.

Asparagine, a health-giving alkaloid found in fresh asparagus, is said to be a healing element for prostate conditions. If you don't have a juicer, find a nearby juice bar and bring in a combination of raw asparagus, carrots and cucumber. Drink a glass of the juice daily.

A teaspoonful of unrefined sesame oil taken every day for one month has been known to reduce an enlarged prostate back to normal.

A warm milk compress is soothing when applied to the prostate area. Warm, do not boil, 1 glass of milk. Saturate a white towel in it and when you apply it to the appropriate area, put a hot water bag on top to keep the towel warmer longer.

Lecithin comes highly recommended from many sources. Take 1 lecithin capsule—1200 mg each—3 times a day, after each meal, or 1 to 2 tablespoonsful of lecithin granules daily.

‡ PROSTATE CONGESTION
If your doctor hasn't already told you, eliminate all coffee and alcoholic beverages from your diet.

And now for a self-help prostatic massage: lie down on the floor on your back. Put the sole of one foot against the sole of the other foot so that you're at your bow-legged best. While keeping the soles of your feet together, extend your legs as far as possible and then bring them in as close as possible to your chest. Do this "extend and bring in" exercise 10 times in the morning and 10 times at night.

‡ PROSTATE PROBLEM PREVENTION
Eat a handful of shelled, unprocessed, unsalted pumpkin seeds each day. The seeds are rich in zinc, magnesium, phosphorus, iron, calcium, protein, unsaturated fatty acid and vitamins A and B-1. There's lots

of research results now supporting the benefits of pumpkin seeds for maintaining prostate health. Start now.

‡ BLOODY URINE AFTER JOGGING

Some men pass bloody urine after jogging. It's usually due to repeated impact of the empty bladder against the prostate. Some doctors recommend that men not empty their bladders completely right before running.

‡ IMPOTENCE (See "Sex.")

‡ PREMATURE EJACULATION (See "Sex.")

‡Memory

"I told my doctor that my memory has gotten terrible lately."

"What did the doctor do about it?"

"He made me pay in advance."

Sure, it's easy to make jokes, but we know how frustrating it is to feel your memory is slipping. A remedy for remembering a familiar name, place or fact, is to simply relax and forget that you can't remember. When you're not thinking about it, it will pop into your mind.

Neither of us believes a good or not so good memory is a matter of age. We think we're all victims of data overload.

Scientist and great logician Albert Einstein didn't believe in remembering anything he could look up. While that's not always practical, it is a tension-relieving thought.

Meanwhile, we have some remedies that may help you recreate a wonderful memory.

Yerba maté (pronounced mah-tay) is a form of holly and is the national beverage of Paraguay, where it's grown. One of the many positive effects of the herb, according to South American medical authorities, is that it strengthens one's memory. Drink 1 cup early in the day (see "Sources").

NOTE: Yerba maté contains caffeine, although less than coffee or regular tea.

Take 1 teaspoonful of apple cider vinegar in a glass of room temperature water before each meal. Not only is it said to be an excellent tonic for the memory, but it also curbs the appetite.

Ah, the healing powers of almonds. Eat 6 raw almonds a day to improve your memory.

Our research led us to a Japanese doctor whose records show that he successfully treated more than 500 patients who were having memory problems. How? Eyebright, the herb best known for treating eye disorders . . . until now. Now we will remember—uh, now we will be able to remember eyebright for restoring one's memory. Add ½ ounce of eyebright and 1 tablespoonful of clover honey to 1½ cups of just-boiled water. When it's cool, strain the mixture and put it in a bottle. Drink ¾ cup before lunch and ¾ cup before dinner.

Two mustard seeds, taken as you would take pills, first thing every morning, are said to revive one's memory.

Eat a handful of sunflower seeds daily. These seeds are beneficial in many ways, one being memory improvement. To get the most flavor out of them, try dry roasting them (see "Preparation Guide").

According to a gem therapist, wearing an amethyst helps strengthen one's memory. You just have to remember to wear the amethyst.

‡Motion Sickness Prevention

Constant jarring of the semicircular canals in the ears causes inner balance problems that produce those awful motion sickness symptoms. To avoid that misery, a doctor at Brigham Young University recommends taking 2 or 3 capsules of powdered ginger root half an hour before the expected motion.

Here's a we-don't-know-why-it-works-but-it-just-seems-to-work remedy: Tape an umeboshi (a Japanese pickled plum) directly on your navel, right before you board a bus, train, car, plane or ship, and it should prevent motion sickness. Umeboshi plums are available at health food stores and at Oriental markets.

Incidentally, the plums are very rich in calcium and iron. Of course to reap those benefits, one must *eat* them, rather than tape them on a tummy.

On any form of transportation, sit near a window so you can look out. Focus on things that are far away, not on nearby objects that move past you quickly.

On a plane, to assure yourself of the smoothest flight possible, select a seat that's over the wheels, not in the tail. There's a lot more movement in the tail end of a plane.

This remedy came to us from Hawaii, Afghanistan and Switzerland. Take a big brown paper bag, cut off and discard the bag's bottom. Then slit the bag from top to bottom so that it's no longer in the round, but instead a long piece of paper. Wrap the paper around your bare chest and secure it in place. Put your regular clothes on top of it and travel that way. It's supposed to prevent motion sickness. Carry another brown paper bag. In case the first one doesn't work, you may need another one.

‡ SEASICKNESS

Marjoram tea is said to help prevent seasickness. Have a cup of the tea before hitting the deck.

Take a teaspoonful of gomasio (sesame seeds and sea salt, available at health food stores) and keep chewing it as long as you can before swallowing it. It should help rid you of that queasy feeling.

‡ JET LAG PREVENTION

Marco Polo, Ferdinand Magellan and Christopher Columbus—all world travelers—but none of them had to worry about jet lag.

There's no question about it, *we* are the "jet lag generation." As a result, our remedies don't go back all that far. As with all our remedies, try the one(s) that make the most sense to you, taking into consideration your own system and how it reacts to things.

This is the U.S. Department of Energy's Anti-Jet Lag Diet to help travelers quickly adjust their bodies' internal clocks to new time zones.

Start 3 days before departure day. Day 1: Have a high-protein breakfast and lunch, and a high-carbohydrate (no meat) dinner. No coffee except between 3 and 5 P.M.

Day 2: Have very light meals—salads, light soups, fruit and juices. Coffee only between 3 and 5 P.M.

Day 3: Same as Day 1.

Day 4, departure: (listen up, this gets complex) If you must have a caffeinated beverage, you can have a cup in the morning when traveling west, or between 6 and 11 P.M. when traveling east. Have fruit or juice until your first meal. To know when to have your first meal, figure out when breakfast time will be at your destination. If your flight is long enough, sleep until normal breakfast time at your destination, *but no later* (that's important). Wake up and eat a big, high-protein breakfast. Stay awake and active. Continue the day's meals according to mealtimes at your destination, and you'll be in sync when you arrive. NO ALCOHOL ON THE PLANE!

This is a modified version of the remedy above that may also help minimize jet lag.

As soon as you board the plane, pretend it's whatever time it actually is at your destination. In other words, if you board the plane at 7:00 P.M. in New York, and and you're headed for London where it's 1:00 A.M., pull down your window shade, or wear dark glasses and, if possible, go to sleep. If you board a plane late that night and it's daylight at your destination, force yourself to stay awake during the flight. Making believe you're in the new time zone at the very start of your trip should help you acclimate quickly.

Princess Diana was given this remedy by William F. Buckley who got it from a world traveler friend of a British doctor specializing in jet lag.

The theory behind the remedy is that jet lag comes from internal perspiring, which causes a salt deficiency. Buckley said that the doctor said to put a heaping teaspoonful of salt in a cup of coffee the minute you get into the plane and drink it. Five hours later, drink another cup and you will experience a miracle. The salted coffee will taste like ambrosia. That is your body talking, telling you how grateful it is that you have given it the salt it so badly needs.

NOTE: This is definitely not for anyone who is watching his or her sodium and/or caffeine intake.

‡Neck Problems

‡ PAIN IN THE NECK
PREVENTION

It's quite common for those of us who are under pressure to have a pain in the neck. People tend to tense up in that area, which is the worst thing to do to yourself. Your neck connects your brain and nervous system to your body. When you create tension in your neck, you impair the flow of energy throughout your system. To prevent tension buildup, do neck rolls. Start with your chin on your chest and slowly rotate your head so that your right ear reaches for your right shoulder, then head back, left ear to left shoulder and back with your chin on your chest. Do these rolls, slowly, 6 times in one direction and 6 times in the opposite direction, morning and evening. You may hear lots of crackling, crunching and gravelly noises coming from your neck. As tension is released, the noises will quiet. See the next remedy to help rid yourself of gravel.

‡ NECK GRAVEL

If, when you roll your neck around, or just turn from side to side, you hear and feel that there's gravel in your neck, do the exercise described above, and eat 3 to 4 cloves of raw garlic a day. You may have to work your way up to that amount. (See "Preparation Guide" for the easiest way to take raw garlic cloves.)

‡ STIFF NECK

Medicine men from several American Indian tribes prescribe daily neck rubs with fresh lemon juice, as well as drinking the juice of half a lemon first thing in the morning and last thing at night.

According to the ancient therapy of reflexology, the base of the big toe affects the neck. Rub your hands together vigorously until you feel heat. Now you're ready to massage your big toes with circular motions. Spend a few minutes massaging the base of the toe and the area surrounding it. As a change of pace, you might want to massage the base of your thumbs, also for a few minutes at a time. Keep at it, at least 2 times a day, every day.

‡ WHIPLASH

Whiplash is the result of neck muscles that were too tense to absorb a sudden thrust. We've been told by

medical professionals that neck collars are the worst thing you can use for whiplash. They don't help realign the neck and they don't let the body help realign itself. A naturopath, chiropractor or osteopath can realign the neck vertebrae. During this uncomfortable time, wear a silk scarf. It has been known to help blood circulation and relieve muscle pain and tension in the neck.

‡Nervous Tension, Anxiety and Stress

Sweaty palms, indigestion, hyperventilating, a stiff neck, an ulcer, a dry mouth, a tic, yes, even a canker sore can be caused by nervous tension, anxiety and stress.

There are as many symptoms and outward manifestations of anxiety as there are reasons for it. Throughout this book, we address ourselves to the problem at hand, like sweaty palms. In this chapter, we address ourselves to the problem that may have caused the symptom: nervous tension, anxiety and stress.

Dr. Joyce Brothers unwinds by doing heavy gardening on her farm. Sailing is a great release for Walter Cronkite. Lawyer F. Lee Bailey pilots his own plane for relaxation.

While not all of us have a plane, a sailboat, or a farm, most of us have a kitchen, a neighborhood health food store and the following tension-relieving remedies:

A good first step would be to get off products with caffeine. Substitute herbal teas for regular tea and coffee. If you're a chocoholic, check out carob bars when you get a craving for chocolate. Health food stores have a big selection of carob treats that have no caffeine. The taste and texture of some carob brands are very similar to chocolate.

Harried housewives, *do not* paint your kitchens yellow to cheer you up. According to color therapist Carlton

Wagner a yellow room contributes to stress and adds to feelings of anxiety.

Here's a little acupressure to relieve life's pressure. For at least 5 minutes a day, massage the webbed area between your thumb and index finger of your left hand. Really get in there and knead it. It may hurt. That's all the more reason to keep at it. Gradually, the pain will decrease, so will the tenseness and tightness in your chest and shoulders. Eventually, you should have no pain at all and you should notice a difference in your general relaxed state of well being.

For a burst of energy without the tension that's usually attached to it, add ⅛ teaspoonful of cayenne pepper to a cup of warm water, and drink it down. It's strong stuff and may take a while to get used to, but cayenne is so beneficial, it's worth it.

Make 2 poultices out of a large, raw, grated onion. Place one poultice on each of your calves and leave it there for half an hour. We know, it's hard to believe that onions on your legs can eliminate nervous anxiety, but don't knock it until you try it.

If all your tension is preventing you from falling asleep, try the tranquilizing effect of a hop pillow. (See "Sleep" for details.)

Let's talk about something lots of you already know about—Valium. Did you know that breast enlargement has been reported in men due to taking Valium? Unfortunately, that's not one of the side effects for women. Oh, but there are some side effects for women. And, there is an alternative that is said to have no side effects. It's called valerian root, the natural forerunner to Valium. Capsules and tablets are available at health food stores. Follow the dosage on the label. Cut and powdered valerian root is available, but the smell is so vile, we can't imagine anyone wanting to make their own tea with it.

Did you know there's a Center for the Interaction of Animals and Society? Well, there is and it's at the University of Pennsylvania where results of a study showed that looking at fish in a home aquarium is as beneficial as biofeedback and meditation, in terms of relaxation techniques. Yup, just sitting in front of a medium-size fish tank, watching ordinary, nonexotic little fish, relaxed people to the point of considerably improving their blood pressure.
Get a few guppies and pull up a chair!

Chia seeds are a calmative. Drink a cup of chia seed tea before each meal. Also sprinkle the seeds on salads.

Alternate nostril breathing is a well-known yoga technique used to put people in a relaxed state with a feeling of inner peace.

Pay attention; it sounds more complex than it is. Place your right thumb against your right nostril. Place your right ring finger and right pinky against your left nostril. (This is not an excercise for anyone with a stuffed nose.) Inhale and slowly exhale through both nostrils. Now, press your right nostril closed and slowly inhale deeply through your left nostril to the count of 5. While your right nostril is still closed, press your left nostril closed. With the air in your lungs, count to 5. Open your right nostril and exhale to the count of 5. Inhale through your right nostril to the count of 5. Close both nostrils and count to 5. Exhale through the left nostril to the count of 5. Keep repeating this pattern for—you guessed it—5 minutes. Do it in the morning when you start your day and at day's end.

Kombu is a seaweed. Kombu tea can be a potent nerve tonic. Add a 3-inch strip of kombu to a quart of water and boil it for 10 minutes. Drink ½ cup at a time throughout the day. Kombu is available at health food stores and Oriental markets.

Do you still have spring clothespins hanging around? Take a handful of them and clip them to the tips of your fingers, at around the start of your nails, of your left hand. Keep them there for 7 minutes. Then put those clothespins on the fingers of your right hand for another 7 minutes. Pressure exerted on nerve endings is known to relax the entire nervous system.

Do this clothespin bit first thing in the morning, and before, during or right after a particularly tense situation.

Goldenseal, an herb, is a calmative and seems especially effective for nervous stomachs. Add ¼ teaspoonful to 1 cup of just-boiled water. Stir well. Drink ½ cup at a time, before each meal and at bedtime.

Here's a visualization exercise used by hypnotherapists and at many self-help seminars. Make sure you're not going to be disturbed by telephones, doorbells, dogs, whistling teapots, etc. Sit in a comfortable chair. Close your eyes. Wait! Read this first, then close your eyes. Once your eyes are closed, put all your awareness in your toes. Feel as though nothing else exists but your toes. Completely relax the muscles in your toes. Slowly move up from your toes to your feet, ankles, calves, knees, thighs, genital area, hips, back, stomach, chest, shoulders, arms, hands, neck, jaw, mouth, cheeks, ears, eyes and brow. Yes, even relax the muscles of your scalp. Now that you're totally relaxed, go get 'em!

‡ STAGE FRIGHT

Most of us get nervous when we have to do any kind of public speaking. In fact, lots of professional performers get a bad case of butterflies before the curtain goes up.

Here are a couple of exercises that can make nervousness a thing of the past.

Before "showtime," stand squarely in front of an immovable wall. Put both your palms on the wall, elbows bent slightly, have your right foot a step in front of the left one, also both legs slightly bent at the knees, and PUSH! PUSH! PUSH! the wall. This flexing of your diaphragm somehow dispels the butterflies.

Remind me to tell you about the time my sister thought

a TV studio wall was immovable and it turned out to be part of a set that was quite movable. (That's one show where we probably won't be invited back.)

A minute before "You're on!" slowly take a deep breath. When no more air will fit into your lungs, hold it for 2 seconds, then let the air out *very fast*, in one big "whoosh." Do this 2 times in a row, and you should be ready to go out there in complete control.

‡Neuralgia

The average human body has 45 miles of nerves.
Neuralgia is an inflammation of a nerve and seems to be caused by poor circulation—too much or too little blood in an area.

To ease the pain of a neuralgia attack, hard boil an egg. Quickly take off the shell, cut the egg in half and immediately apply both halves to the trouble spot. By the time the egg cools, the pain should be gone.

If you have neuralgic pains in the face, let the hot streams of a shower beat against the problem area. Or, you might want to try a hot water compress if you feel that the shower is too much for you to take.

‡Nosebleeds

Do not lie down. Always keep your head elevated.

NOTE: Nasal hemorrhaging—blood flowing from both nostrils—requires immediate medical attention. Rush to the nearest doctor.

Recurrent nosebleeds may be a symptom of an underlying ailment. Seek appropriate medical attention.

In our first book, we reported that a small piece of brown paper from a brown paper bag, placed between the upper lip and the gum, has been known to stop a bloody nose in no time. We have since heard that a dime under the upper lip also stops the nosebleed. If you're outdoors without a paper bag or a dime, a stiff green leaf from a tree can serve the purpose. Place the leaf under your upper lip and press down on it with your finger.

This is a remedy that came to us from the Caribbean Islands: Take the pinky finger of the hand opposite the bleeding nostril and tightly tie a string under the pinky's fingernail. It must work. Have you ever seen anyone on those Jamaica commercials with a bloody nose?

We know that cayenne pepper stops the bleeding of a cut or gash. We've been told that drinking ⅛ teaspoonful of cayenne in a glass of warm water will stop a nosebleed.

Gem therapists say that a nosebleed can be stopped by placing a piece of pure amber on the nose.

If you happen to get a bloody nose right before making chicken soup, take a piece of the fresh raw chicken and insert it up the bleeding nostril. What we would like to know is, how in the world someone ever discovered this to be an effective remedy for a nosebleed. If you know, please let us know.

Vinegar is said to be very helpful in getting a bloody nose under control. Pour some vinegar on a cloth and wash the neck, nose and temples with it. Also, mix 2 teaspoonsful in half a glass of warm water and drink it.

‡ PREVENTING NOSEBLEEDS
Bioflavonoids help prevent nosebleeds. Eat at least one citrus fruit a day and be sure to include the white rubbery skin under the peel. It's called the "pith" and it's extremely rich in bioflavonoids.

‡Phlebitis

If you know you have phlebitis, chances are you are under a doctor's care and should be. Check with your doctor about the following suggestions. We're certain (s)he will agree that these cannot harm you. And they sure as heck can help dissolve blood clots!

Apply a comfrey poultice on the outside of the affected area.

You should be on a raw vegetable diet. It's important to have sprouts and leafy greens, plus lots more roughage.

Also, drink lots of fresh juices.

Take 1 tablespoonful of lecithin every day.

And surely your doctor told you to elevate the affected area as many hours a day as possible.

‡Ringworm

A woman called us to share her ringworm remedy:
mix blue fountain pen ink with cigar ashes and put the
mixture on the fungus-infected area. The woman said
she has never seen it to fail. Within a few days the
ringworm completely disappears.

If this remedy is going to get you into the habit of
smoking cigars, stick with the ringworm, or try the next
remedy.

Mince or grate garlic and mix it with an equal amount
of vaseline. Apply the mixture to the trouble spots and
cover with gauze. Leave it that way overnight.
Throughout the day, puncture garlic perles and rub the
oil on the afflicted areas. The garlic should stop the
itching and help heal the rash.

‡Sciatica

Sciatica is a painful condition affecting the sciatic nerve, which is the longest nerve in the body. It extends from the lower spine through the pelvis, thighs, down into the legs and ends at the heels. We all have some nerve!

Polish folk healers tell their patients who suffer from sciatica to wear long woolen underwear, red only, and carry a raw beet in their hip pocket.

We heard about a man who went from doctor to doctor for help. None helped. As a last resort, the man followed the advice of a folk medicine practitioner who recommended garlic milk. The man minced 2 cloves of garlic, put them in ½ cup of milk and drank it down (without chewing the pieces of garlic). He had the garlic milk each morning and each evening. Within a few days, he felt some relief. Within 2 weeks, all the pain had completely disappeared.

Water has tremendous therapeutic value for a sciatic condition. It can reduce the pain and improve circulation. Take a long, hot bath or shower and follow it with a short cold shower. If you can't stand the thought of a cold shower, then follow up the hot bath with ice cold compresses on the painful areas.

‡ Sex

While we did have "Impotence" under "Male Problems," and "Frigidity" under "Female Problems" in our first folk remedy book, we did not include the subject of "Sex."

During appearances on dozens of radio and television shows, we were constantly asked sex-related questions. As a result, in this book we decided to give the people what they want—more sex! That is, remedies for sexual dysfunctions and some fuel to help rev up the sex drive.

Researchers tell us that about 90 percent of the cases of decreased sexual ability are psychologically caused. Since a psychological placebo has been known to evoke a prize-winning performance, we're including rituals, recipes, potions, lotions, charms and all kinds of passion-promoting spells.

For history buffs and for history in the buff, we culled the ancient Greek, Egyptian, Indian and Oriental sex secrets that are still being used today.

So, if you did but don't; should but won't; can't but want to; or, do but don't enjoy it, please read on. Help and new-found-fun may be waiting on the following pages.

‡ FOR MEN ONLY

‡ Impotence: Organic or Psychological?—A Test

Most men have about 5 erections every night in their sleep. No matter how uptight they might be, and no matter what trouble they might be having with erections while awake, men who suffer from psychological impotency will have firm erections every night in their sleep.

To test for these erections, get a roll of postage stamps (any denomination) and wrap it in a single thickness around the shaft of the penis. Tear off the excess stamps, then tape the 2 ends (the first and the last stamps) around the penis, firmly but not too tight. Pleasant dreams!

When a nighttime erection occurs, the increased diameter of the penis should break the stamps along the line of one of the perforations. If impotency is organically caused, you will not have nightly erections and the stamps will be intact in the morning.

The "stamp act" should be repeated every night for 3 to 4 weeks. If, each morning, the stamps are broken along a perforation, chances are you have a normal capability for having erections and impotency is psychologically caused. Sometimes just knowing that everything is working well organically will give you the confidence and assurance you need to help you rise to the occasion.

‡ The Fear of Failure

In the Mexican pharmacopoeia, damiana is classified as an aphrodisiac and a tonic for the nervous system. It's been known to be an effective remedy for "performance anxiety."

Add a teaspoonful of damiana leaves to a cup of just-boiled water. Let it steep for 10 minutes. Strain and drink before breakfast, on a daily basis (see "Sources").

‡ Amazonico Impotence Remedy

El Indio Amazonico, a Bogota botanico (medicine man), advises his impotent patients to not even try to

have sex for 30 days. During that time, he suggests they eat goat meat every day, in addition to bulls' testicles ("mountain oysters"). He also recommends drinking tea made of cinnamon sticks and cups of cocoa. When the abstention period is over, El Indio instructs his patients to rub a small amount of petroleum jelly mixed with a bit of lemon juice around—but not on—the scrotum. Then they're on their own.

‡ Love Longer

Eat a handful of raw, hulled pumpkin seeds every day. (The cooking process may destroy some of the special values of the seeds, so steer clear of the roasted ones.) Pumpkin seeds contain large amounts of zinc, magnesium, iron, phosphorus, calcium, vitamin A and the B vitamins. According to a West German medical researcher, there are one or more substances not yet isolated that have vitalizing and regenerative effects and actually cause additional sex hormones to be produced. Many health authorities agree that a handful of pumpkin seeds a day can help prevent prostate problems and impotence. Pass the pumpkin seeds!

‡ Voice and Vitality

It is said that the higher a man's voice, the lower his masculine vitality. The theory is based on the fact that the vortex at the base of the neck and the vortex in the sex center are directly connected and affected by each other. Men, lower your voice and you'll increase the speed of vibration in these vortexes, which, in turn, may increase your sexual energy.

‡ Recipe for Sexual Stamina

Hindi records, circa tenth century, tell about men who went to view the famous Temple of Khajuraho in India to study its pornographic stone carvings depicting every known position of love. For stamina to test the positions, they were fed this eggplant dish:

Slice an eggplant and cover with butter and minced chives on both sides. Brown the slices and cover with a spicy curry sauce.

The recipe (unspecific as it is) has been passed down from generation to generation, along with its reputation for making old men young again.

‡ Stay out of Hot Water

Fast cold showers do not cool or dampen one's sexual desire. Au contraire! Short applications of cold water, particularly on the nape of the neck, are sexually stimulating.

‡ Stronger Erection

Most men get a stronger erection and feel more of a sensation when their bladder is full. However, some positions may be uncomfortable if it's very full.

NOTE: Men with prostate problems should not practice this technique.

‡ **Premature Ejaculation**

According to sex therapists, premature ejaculation seems to be one of the easiest conditions to cure, simply by behavior modification. This is Masters and Johnson's conditioning treatment: Enlist the assistance of your mate who should be very willing to comply. Lie on your back with your legs straddling your partner. Have her stimulate your penis until you feel that orgasm is just around the corner. At that second, give her a prearranged signal. In response to the signal, she should stop stimulating and start squeezing the penis just below the tip. She should squeeze it firmly enough to cause you to lose your erection, but not to cause you pain. When the feeling that you are about to ejaculate leaves you, have her stimulate you again. As before, signal her when orgasm is imminent and, once again, she should stop stimulating and start squeezing the penis. The erection should go down and you will not ejaculate. Keep this up (and down) for a while and soon you will be able to control ejaculation.

The next step is intercourse. As soon as you feel you are about to climax, signal your partner, withdraw from her and have her squeeze your penis until you lose the erection. Practice makes perfect. Masters and Johnson have reported that in just 2 weeks of using this behavior modification program, 98 percent of men with premature ejaculation are cured.

‡ **The Heart and the Heat of Passion**

It's a myth that sex is dangerous to the heart, according to Dr. Richard A. Stein, director of the heart exercise laboratory at the State University of New York Downstate Medical Center.

The stress to the heart is really very mild. The average heart rate increases up to 115–120 beats per minute during intercourse—a muscle workload equal to walking up two flights of stairs.

If a man is cheating on his mate, the heart rate and risk rises with the excitement and the danger of being caught.

‡ FOR WOMEN ONLY

‡ Overcome Frigidity

In Greek mythology, Anaxarete was so cold to her suitors . . . How cold was she? She was so cold, that Venus, the Goddess of Love, turned her into a marble statue. That's cold!

Here is an antifreeze that might work even for Anaxarete: Boil 1 cup of finely minced chive leaves and roots with 2 cups of champagne. Then simmer until reduced to a thick cupful. Drink it unstrained. It's no wonder this syrup may work. Centuries later, we learned it's rich in vitamin E (the love vitamin). Also, champagne has always been known to provoke passion. Casanova used it continually in his erotic cookery.

‡ Heighten a Man's Orgasm

Touching the testicles before his orgasm is a wonderful way for a woman to greatly excite her lover. It also may hasten as well as heighten the orgasm.

NOTE: Touching the testicles just after orgasm is a no-no. It gives an unpleasant, almost painful sensation.

‡ Love Elixir for Sexual Responsiveness

Ancient Teuton brides drank honey-beer for the 30 days after their wedding ceremony. It was said to make the bride more sexually responsive. The custom of honey-beer for a month, poetically referred to as a "moon," is the way we got the term, "honeymoon."

Rather than go through the big bother of preparing honey-beer the way they did way back when, herbalists simplified it to a tea made from hops and honey.

Place 1 ounce of hops in a porcelain or Pyrex container. Pour 1 pint of boiling water over the hops, cover and allow it to stand for 15 minutes, then strain. Add a teaspoonful of raw honey to a wineglassful of tea and drink it an hour before each meal. If you prefer warm hops and honey, heat the tea before drinking.

Honey has aspartic acid and vitamin E. Honey and hops contain traces of hormones. All these ingredients are said to stimulate female sexuality. I'll drink to that!

‡ It Makes Scents
Have your favorite fragrance linger in the air and help set the mood for romance. Lightly spray your perfume on a light bulb—one you plan to leave on. In cold weather, spray your radiator too.

‡ Fertili-Tea

Add 1 teaspoonful of sarsaparilla to 1 cup of just-boiled water and let it steep for 5 minutes. Strain and drink 2 cups a day.

While sarsaparilla tea may be helpful to a woman who wants to conceive, it should not be given to a man who wants to be potent. Sarsaparilla seems to inhibit the formation of sperm.

‡ Fertility Charm

Hundreds of years ago, witches wore necklaces of acorns to symbolize the fertile powers of nature. In some circles it is still believed that by carrying an acorn you will promote sexual relations and conception.

‡ Muscle Strengthener

The ancient Japanese, masters of sensuality, invented Ben Wa Balls. Later, eighteenth century French women referred to them as "pommes d'amour." When these brass balls (or, sometimes gold-plated steel) are placed in the vagina, they create a stimulating sensation upon the vaginal wall muscles. Doctors throughout the world have recommended them for their therapeutic value (see "Sources").

‡ FOR MEN AND WOMEN

‡ Time for Love

Testosterone, the sexual desire-stimulating hormone, is at its lowest level in the body at bedtime, 11

P.M. It's at its highest level at sunrise. No wonder you may not want to make love during *The Tonight Show*. Instead, try getting up with the roosters, and maybe you and your mate will have something to crow about.

‡ Tea for Two

Turkish women believe fenugreek tea makes them more attractive to men. Besides the sexual energy it may give them, the tea has a way of cleansing the system, sweetening the breath and helping eliminate perspiration odors.

Men suffering from the lack of desire and/or inability to perform, have turned to fenugreek tea with success.

Many men with sexual problems lack vitamin A. Fenugreek contains an oil that's rich in vitamin A. Trimethylamine, another substance found in fenugreek, and currently being tested on men, acts as a sex hormone in frogs. If you want to do your own testing, add 2 teaspoonsful of fenugreek seeds to a cup of just-boiled water. Let it steep for 5 minutes, stir, strain, add honey and lemon to taste. Drink a cup a day and don't be surprised if you get the urge to make love on a lily pad.

‡ Sexy Clam Bake

Bake the meat of a dozen clams for about 2 hours at 400 degrees. When the clam meat is dark and hard, take out of oven, let cool and pulverize it to a powder, either in a blender or with a mortar and pestle. Take ½ teaspoonful of the clam powder with water, 2 hours before bedtime, for 1 week. This Japanese folk remedy is supposed to restore sexual vitality.

‡ Aphrodisiacs

We heard about a married couple whose idea of "sexual compatibility" is for both of them to get a headache at the same time.

They're the ones who asked us to include aphrodisiacs. The word itself means "any form of sexual stimulation." It was derived from Aphrodite, the Goddess of Love, who earned her title by having one husband and five lovers including that handsome Greek guy, Adonis. Enough about her!

Here are recipes for you and your mate that can add new vigor and uninhibited sensuality to your love life.

‡ Sensation Stirrer

To get in the mood, get in a warm bath to which you've added 2 drops of jasmine oil, 2 drops of ylang-ylang oil and 8 drops of sandalwood oil. These essential oils are natural, organic substances that work in harmony with the natural forces of the body. Health food stores carry these "oils of olé!" You might want to save water by bathing together.

‡ The Curse That Renews Sexual Bliss

Ancient mystics used "curses" as a positive way to reverse the negative flow to physical manifestations. In other words, if you're not hot to trot, Curses! The secret of success lies in the emotional charge behind the incantation as you repeat it morning, noon and right before bedtime:

Amor and Psyche, Cupid and Venus, restore to me
   passion and vitality.
Mars and Jupiter, Ares and Zeus, instill in me
   strength and force.
Lusty waters and penetrating winds, renew my
   vigor, my capacity, my joy.
Cursed be weakness, cursed be shyness,
Cursed be impotence, cursed be frigidity,
Cursed be all that parts me and thee!

‡ Passion Fruit

Fruits beginning with the letter "p" are said to be
especially good for increasing potency in men and en-
hancing sexual energy in women. The fruits we recommend are: peaches, plums, pears, pineapple, pa-
payas, persimmons and don't forget bananas—uh,
pananas.

‡ Potion and Chant for Enduring Love

Stir a pinch of ground coriander seeds into a glass of
fine red wine while repeating this chant together:

Warm and caring heart
Let us never be apart.

Both drink the wine from the same glass, taking turns. When the wine is all gone, your love should be here to stay.

‡ American Indian Passion Promoter

Add 2 tablespoonsful of unrefined oatmeal and ½ cup of raisins to 1 quart of water and bring it to a boil. Reduce heat, cover tightly and simmer slowly for 45 minutes. Remove from heat and strain. Add the juice of 2 lemons and stir in honey to taste. Refrigerate the mixture. Drink 2 cups a day—1 before breakfast and another an hour before bedtime.

Oatmeal is rich in vitamin E. Is that where "sow wild oats" comes from?

‡ A Gem of a Gem

According to a gem therapist, turquoise is said to increase its owner's sexual drive.

‡ The Honeymoon Picker-Upper

This is an updated recipe of an ancient Druid formula. Sex therapists who prescribe it believe that taking it on a regular basis can generate a hearty sexual appetite.

Mix the following ingredients in a blender for several seconds: 2 level tablespoonsful of skim milk powder and water according to the skim milk instructions, ¼ teaspoonful of powdered ginger, ⅛ teaspoonful of powdered cinnamon, 4 tablespoonsful of raw honey and a dash of lemon juice, plus any fresh fruit or pure fruit juice you care to add.

You and your mate should drink this picker-upper at least 20 minutes before bedtime.

‡ The Ultimate Aphrodisiac

There is no elixir, tonic, brew, herb, oil or food that can surpass the power of the ultimate aphrodisiac: a desirable partner passionately asking to be enjoyed.

‡Skin

Skin is the largest organ of the body. The average adult has 17 square feet of skin. Thick or thin skinned, it weighs about 5 pounds.

Five pounds of skin covering 17 square feet of body surface . . . that's a lot of room for eruptions, rashes, scrapes, scratches, splinters, wrinkles, sores and enlarged pores.

Gimme some skin and we'll give you some remedies!

‡ ACNE

The following acne remedies may not produce dramatic results overnight. Select one and stay with it for at least two weeks. If there's no improvement by then, go on to another remedy.

Take ⅓ cup uncooked oats and, in a blender, pulverize them into a powder. Then add water—a little less than ⅓ cup—so that it becomes the consistency of paste. Apply the paste to the pimples. Leave this soothing and healing mush on until it dries up and starts crumbling off. Wash it all off with tepid water.

NOTE: Always wash your face with tepid water. Hot water can cause the breaking of capillaries, as can cold water.

Using a juice extractor, juice 1 cucumber. With a pastry brush, apply the cucumber juice to the trouble spots. Leave it on for at least 15 minutes, then wash off with tepid water.

Boil ⅓ cup of buttermilk. While it's hot, add enough honey to the buttermilk to make it a thick creamy consistency. With a pastry brush, brush the cooled mixture on the acned area. Leave it on for at least 15 minutes. Wash off with tepid water.

This is an industrial-strength acne remedy taken internally. Before breakfast, or as your breakfast, on the first day, start with 2 teaspoonsful of brewer's yeast, 1 tablespoonful of lecithin granules and 1 tablespoonful of cold pressed safflower oil, all in 1 glass of pure apple juice. On the second day, add another teaspoonful of brewer's yeast and another teaspoonful of lecithin granules. Each day, add another teaspoonful of brewer's yeast and lecithin granules until you're taking 2 tablespoonsful (6 teaspoonsful) of brewer's yeast and the same amount of lecithin, along with the 1 tablespoonful of safflower oil, all in 1 glass of apple juice. As this detoxifies your system and rids you of acne, it should give you added energy and shiny hair. It is advisable to do this only with medical supervision.

‡ BROWN SPOTS (LIVER SPOTS, AGE SPOTS)

The following remedies may not produce instant results. These brown spots, thought to be caused by a nutrition deficiency, took years to form. Give the remedy you use a few months to work. Then, if there's no change, change remedies.

Grate an onion and squeeze it through cheesecloth so that you have 1 teaspoonful of onion juice. Mix it with 2 teaspoonsful of vinegar and massage the brown spots with this liquid. Do it daily—twice a day if possible—until you no longer see spots in front of your eyes.

This Israeli remedy calls for chick peas. You may know them as garbanzo beans, ceci, or arbus. If you don't want to prepare them from scratch, buy canned chick peas. Mash about ⅓ cupful and add a little water. Smear the paste on the brown spots and leave it there till it dries and starts crumbling off. Then wash it off completely. Do this every evening.

Once a day, take 1 vitamin E capsule (400 I.U.) orally. In addition, at bedtime, puncture an E capsule, squish out the oil and rub it on the brown spots, leaving it on overnight.

A variation of this remedy is to rub on castor oil and still take the vitamin E orally.

‡ BOILS

Mix 1 tablespoonful of honey with 1 tablespoonful of cod liver oil (Norwegian emulsified cod liver oil is nonsmelly) and glob it on the boil. Bind it with a sterile bandage. Change the dressing every 8 hours.

To draw out the waste material painlessly and quickly, add a little water to about 1 teaspoonful of fenugreek powder, making it the consistency of paste. Put it on the boil and cover it with a sterile bandage. Change the dressing twice a day.

This Irish remedy requires 4 slices of bread and a cup of milk. Boil the bread and milk together until it's one big gloppy mush. As soon as the mush is cool enough to handle, slop a glop on the boil and cover with a sterile bandage. When the glop gets cold, replace it with another warm glop. Keep redressing the boil until you've used up all 4 slices of bread. By then, the boil should have opened.

‡ WHEN THE BOIL BREAKS

The boil is at the brink of breaking when it turns red and the pain increases. When it finally does break, pus will be expelled, leaving a temporary opening in the skin. Almost magically, the pain will disappear. Boil 1 cup of water and add 2 tablespoonsful of lemon juice. Let it cool. Clean and disinfect the area thoroughly with the lemon water. Cover with a sterile bandage. For the next few days, 2 or 3 times a day, remove the bandage and apply a warm, wet compress, leaving it on for 15 minutes. Re-dress the area with a fresh sterile bandage.

‡ BRUISES

Grate a piece of turnip, or a piece of daikon (Japanese radish). Apply the grated root to the bruise and leave it there for 15 to 30 minutes. These two roots have been known to help clean up the internal bleeding of the bruise.

Spread a thin layer of blackstrap molasses on a piece of brown (grocery bag) paper and apply the molasses side to the bruise. Bind it in place and leave it there for hours.

Peel a banana and apply the inside of the banana skin to the bruise. It will lessen the pain and reduce the discoloration. Bind the skin in place with a cold, wet bandage.

Mix 2 tablespoonsful of cornstarch with 1 tablespoonful of castor oil. Dampen a clean white cloth and make a cornstarch/castor oil paste poultice. Apply the poultice to the bruise and leave it on until the damp cloth gets dry.

‡ HIVES
Hives usually disappear almost as fast and as mysteriously as they appear. If yours are hanging on, rub them with buckwheat flour. That ought to teach 'em to hang around!

Combine 3 tablespoonsful of cornstarch and 1 tablespoonful of vinegar. Mix well and apply the paste to the hives.

‡ ITCHING (PRURITIS)

Rub the itchy area with a slice of raw potato, or grate the raw potato and use it as a poultice. It has the power to pull out the itchiness.

To stop an itch, wash the itchy part with strong rum. This remedy is from—where else?—Jamaica.

Do you have a drawstring bag made of cotton? You can sew one easily, using a white handkerchief. Fill the bag with 1 pound of uncooked oatmeal and close it tightly. Throw it in your tub as you run the warm bath water. Then, take a bath and, with the oatmeal-filled bag, gently massage the dry itchy skin. Enjoy staying in the bath for at least 15 minutes.

‡ RECTAL ITCHING

Itching around the "tush" may be caused by intestinal parasites. It sounds worse than it is. For years, pumpkin seeds have been used as a folk treatment to control and prevent intestinal bacteria. Buy the shelled and unsalted seeds, then dry roast them by placing them in an enamel pan over the fire. In a couple of minutes, they'll start popping up. It's fun. Eat a handful of pumpkin seeds daily.

‡ GENITAL ITCHING

Sprinkle cornstarch all over the itching area.

Buttermilk is known to stop the itching and help heal the area. Dip a cotton pad in some buttermilk and apply it to the problem spot.

‡ POISON IVY

Try hard not to scratch the rash. That's easy for us to say. Wash with soap and water. Then, put pieces of tofu (the white puffy little soybean-processed pillows sold at greengrocers) directly on each rash, and bind them in place. It should stop the itching and cool off the poison ivy flare-up.

Don't be a crab, just get one. Try either remedy: boil the whole crab in water and use the water to wash the poison ivy area. Or, look inside the crab shell for the green stuff. Apply that green guck directly on the rash.

‡ SHAVING RASH

Men, ever get a shaving rash, particularly on your neck? Women, all we need to say are two words: bikini area.

Puncture a vitamin E capsule, squish out the contents and mix it with a little petroleum jelly. Then, gently spread the mixture on the irritated skin.

Cornstarch makes a soothing powder for underarms and other rash-ridden areas.

‡ HEAT RASH (PRICKLY HEAT)

Make a soothing powder by browning ½ cup of regular flour in the oven.

Rub the prickly heated area with the inside of watermelon rind.

‡ PSORIASIS

Some people respond very well to this remedy. It's certainly worth a try. Add 1 teaspoonful of sarsaparilla root (see "Sources") to 1 cup of just-boiled water and let it steep for 15 minutes. If it's cool enough by then, strain and saturate a white washcloth in the liquid and apply it to the trouble spot. You may need more than one washcloth, depending on the extent of the condition.

‡ SHINGLES

We heard how buckbean worked for a shingles sufferer when nothing else would. He made a tea by adding 1 ounce of the dried buckbean leaves to 2 cups of water and letting it steep for 10 minutes. Each day he took 4 tablespoonsful of the tea before each meal. Within a short time, he was fine and able to return to work.

Until you get the buckbean (see the remedy above), you might want to make a paste of baking soda and water, and apply it to the affected area for some relief.

‡ HARD-TO-HEAL SORE AND LESION

Some nonmalignant sores need help healing. Put pure, undiluted Concord grape juice on a sterilized cotton puff or gauze pad, and apply it to the sore, binding it in place with a bandage. Do not wash the sore. Just keep the grape juice on it, changing the dressing at least once in the morning and once at night. Be patient. It may take 2 to 3 weeks for the sore to heal.

‡ SPLINTERS

Make a poultice from the grated heart of a cabbage. Apply it to the splinter and in an hour or 2, it should draw the sliver out.

For real tough splinters, sprinkle salt on the splintered area, then put half a cherry tomato on it. Easy on the mayo! (Only kidding.) Bind the tomato on the salted skin with a bandage and a plastic covering to keep from messing up the bed linen. Oh, we forgot to mention, you're supposed to sleep with the tomato overnight. (Now, now, fellas!) The next morning, the splinter should come right out.

‡ Warts

Every day, apply a poultice of blackstrap molasses and keep it on the wart as long as possible. You should also eat a tablespoonful of molasses daily. In about 2 weeks, the wart should drop off without leaving a trace.

We heard about a young woman who used an old remedy. She applied regular white chalk to the wart every night. On the sixth night, the wart fell off. She was able to chalk it up to experience.

In the morning and in the evening, rub the wart with one of the following:

a radish
juice of marigold flowers
bacon rind
oil of cinnamon
wheat germ oil
a thick paste of buttermilk and
   baking soda

‡ Warts on Hand
Boil eggs and save the water. As soon as it's cool, soak your warted hand(s) in that water for 10 minutes. Do it daily until the warts disappear.

‡ Plantar Warts
Plantar warts are the kind you find on the soles of the feet, usually in clusters. It starts as a little black dot. Don't pick it; you'll only make it spread. Instead, rub castor oil on it every night until it's history.

‡ FACE CARE
The first thing to ask yourself is: "What kind of skin do I have—dry, oily, combination or normal?" If you're not sure, Heloise, the helpful hints lady, has a test you can take.

"Wash your face with shaving cream. Rinse. Wait about three hours so that your skin can revert to its regular self. Then take cigarette papers or any other thin tissue paper and press pieces of it on your face."

If it sticks, leaving an oily spot that's visible when you hold it up to the light, you've got oily skin. If it doesn't stick, your skin is dry. If it sticks, but doesn't leave oily spots, you've got normal skin. If the papers stick on some areas, leaving oily spots, and don't stick on other areas, you have combination skin.

Now that you know what kind of skin you have, here's how to take care of it.

Always use an upward and outward motion when doing anything to one's face—whether you're washing it, doing a facial, applying makeup or removing makeup.

When you wash your face, use tepid water. Hot or cold water may break the small capillaries—those little red squiggly veins—in your face.

It's important to wash your face 2 times a day or more. Washing removes dead cells, keeps pores clean and skin texture good. The morning wash-up is necessary because of metabolic activity during the night. (*Everyone* has metabolic activity whether they go to singles' bars or not.) The night wash-up is necessary because of all the dirt that piles up during the day. Wash with a mild soap and a washcloth or cosmetic sponge, upward and outward. Now, onward . . .

NOTE: Interspersed on the following pages are masks for oily, dry, normal and combination skin. The best time to apply a mask is at night, when you don't have to put on makeup for at least 6 to 8 hours afterwards.

The best way to apply a mask is after you've taken a bath or shower, or after you've gently steamed your face so that the pores are open.

‡ Care of Oily Skin

Cleansers seem to be a problem for oily skin because of the high alcohol content of most makeup-removing astringents. They're usually too harsh for one's skin on a regular basis. Instead, use 1 teaspoonful of powdered milk with enough warm water to give it a milky consistency. With cotton puffs, apply the liquid to your face and neck, gently rubbing it on. Once you've covered your entire face and neck, remove makeup and dirt with a tissue, again, gently. Pat dry.

Many folk healers suggest drinking a strong cup of yarrow tea, which is an astringent, to cut down on skin oiliness. Use 1 tablespoonful of dried yarrow (see "Sources") in a cup of just-boiled water. Let it steep for 10 minutes. Strain and drink daily.

In a blender, blend ¼ of a small eggplant (skin and all), with 1 cup of plain yogurt. Smear the mush on your face and neck (but *not* on the delicate skin around your eyes), and stay that way for 20 minutes. Rinse with tepid water. Finish this treatment with a nonalcoholic astringent like the yarrow tea in the remedy above. Fill a plastic plant mister with a cup of the tea (camomile is also an astringent and can be used), and spray your face with it. Keep it in the refrigerator so you can use it to set your makeup or to freshen up, as well as a toner, after this eggplant/yogurt mask.

‡ Care of Dry Skin

Instead of using soap and water, clean your face with whole milk. Warm 2 to 3 tablespoonsful of milk, add ½ teaspoonful of castor oil and shake well. Dunk a cotton puff (not a tissue) into the mixture and start

cleaning, using upward and outward strokes. This combination of milk and oil is said to take off more makeup and city dirt than the most expensive professional cleansing products ever could. And it does it naturally, not chemically. Complete the treatment by sealing in moisture with a thin layer of castor oil.

A leading cause of dry skin is towels. (Just checking to see if you're paying attention.)

Avocado is highly recommended for dry skin. You can use the inside of the avocado skin and massage your just-washed face and neck with it. Or, you can mix equal amounts of avocado (about ¼ cup) with sour cream. Gently rub it on the face and neck (but *not* on the delicate skin around the eyes), and leave it there for at least 15 minutes. Rinse with tepid water. When you can no longer see a trace of the mixture, with your fingertips work the invisible oil into your skin with an upward and outward sweep, again, gently.

Another wonderful mask for dry skin is the banana mask. Look for it under "Wrinkle Prevention," later in this chapter.

‡ Care of Combination Skin

Using different masks for the dry and oily parts of your face is a real nuisance. Instead, you may want to try these treatments, good for all types of skin.

This once-a-month cleansing calls for 1 cup of uncooked oatmeal, powdered in a blender. Add 3 drops of almond oil, ½ cup of skim milk and 1 egg white. Blend it all, then spread it on your face and neck (not around your eyes), and let it stay there for half an hour. Rinse it off with tepid water.

This papaya facial helps remove dead skin cells and allows the new skin to breathe freely. Papaya accomplishes naturally what most commercial products do chemically.

In a blender, purée a ripe, peeled papaya. Spread the fruit on your face and neck and keep it there for 20 minutes. Rinse off with tepid water. It would be good to have this facial once or twice a month, but since it's not always possible to get papaya in most areas of the country, do it whenever you can.

This mask is for everyone all year 'round. It's a honey of a honey mask. Folk practitioners claim that it: helps rid the face of blemishes and blackheads; leaves you feeling refreshed and invigorated; restores weather-beaten skin; prevents skin from aging by helping it maintain the normal proportion of water in the skin. The longer we go on, the more the skin is aging. Here's how to apply the mask: Start with a clean face and neck and with your hair out of the way. Dip your fingertips in raw, unheated honey and gently spread it on your face and neck in an upward and outward motion. Leave it on for 20 minutes, then rinse it off with tepid water. It's sweet and simple . . . and sticky.

Wet your clean face and rub on a glob of petroleum jelly. Keep adding water as you thin out the layer of jelly all over your face and neck until it's no longer greasy. This inexpensive treatment is used at expensive spas because it's an effective moisturizer.

One source described this apple cider vinegar treatment as, "The cleansing acid that cuts through residue film and clears the way for healthful complexion breathing." Another source said, "This treatment will restore the acid covering your skin needs for protection." And still another said, "This 'Skin Awakener Formula' is, by far, the simplest natural healer for tired skin. It gives you the glow of fresh-faced and shiny button youth." (That source talks funny.)

Mix 1 tablespoonful of apple cider vinegar with 1 tablespoonful of just-boiled water. As soon as the liquid is cool enough, apply it to the face with cotton puffs. Lydia tried it. It made her skin feel smooth and tight. Her eyes were a little teary from the strong fumes of the diluted vinegar and, for about 10 minutes, she smelled like cole slaw.

Use this treatment often, at least every other day, or whenever you have a craving for cole slaw.

Some people keep a plastic plant mister filled with equal amounts of apple cider vinegar and water to spray their bodies after a shower or bath. It not only restores the acid mantle (pH balance) in the skin, it removes soap residue and hard water deposits, too.

‡ SUN-ABUSED SKIN

Soften that leathery look with this centuries-old beauty mask formula. Mix 2 tablespoonsful of raw honey with 2 tablespoonsful of flour. Add enough milk (2 to 3 tablespoonsful) to make it the consistency of toothpaste.

Be sure your face and neck are clean and your hair is out of the way. Smooth the paste on the face and neck. Stay clear of the delicate skin around the eyes. Leave the paste on for half an hour, rinse it off with tepid water and pat dry. Tone and moisturize.

Now you need a toner. May we make a suggestion? In a juice extractor, juice 2 cucumbers, heat to the boiling point, skim the froth off (if any), bottle the juice and refrigerate it. Twice daily, use 1 teaspoonful of juice to 2 teaspoonsful of water. Gently dab it on your face and neck and let it dry.

Now you need a moisturizer. Consider using a light film of olive oil or castor oil.

‡ FRECKLES

An old antifreckle folk remedy is to wash your face with warm beer. So, if you really want to get rid of those little brown speckles, get the warm beer and hop to it. Repeated washings several days in a row may be necessary. Also, right after the treatment, apply a light film of oil to your skin to prevent irritation of sensitive facial tissues.

If you're determined to do away with your freckles, bottle your own freckle remover. Get 4 medium-size dandelion leaves (either pick them yourself, or buy them at the greengrocer), rinse them thoroughly and tear them into small pieces. Combine the leaves with 5 table-spoonsful of castor oil in an enamel or glass pan over low heat. Let it simmer for 10 minutes. Turn off the heat, cover the pan and let it steep for 3 hours. Strain the mixture into a bottle. (Don't forget to label the bottle.) Massage several drops of the oil on the befreck-led area and leave it on overnight. In the morning, wash your face with tepid water. Do this daily for at least a week and watch the spots disappear.

If by now you're desperate to get rid of those freckles of yours, take a glass of your morning urine and mix it with a tablespoonful of apple cider vinegar. Add a pinch of salt and let it stand for 24 hours. Next, put it on the freckles for a half hour, then rinse with cool water and follow it with a soothing oil. To get results, you will most likely have to do this several times. Are you sure you really don't want freckles?

Incidentally, urine has been used as an effective folk medicine for centuries. In our first folk remedy book, we wrote about a miracle acne cure using urine after everything else failed.

‡ ENLARGED PORES
So you have some enlarged pores. Think of it this way: in our 17 square feet of skin, we have about one

billion pores. Percentage-wise, look how few are en-larged.

To help refine those pores, put ⅓ cup of almonds into a blender and pulverize them into a powder. Add enough water to the powder to give it the consistency of paste. Rub the mixture gently across the enlarged pores from your nose outward and upward. Leave it on your face for half an hour, then rinse it off with tepid water. As a final rinse, mix ¼ cup of cool water with ¼ cup of apple cider vinegar and splash it on to tighten the pores.

You will have to treat your skin to this almond rub on a regular basis to get results.

‡ WRINKLES

We know a man who has so many wrinkles in his forehead, he has to screw his hat on. That's a lot of wrinkles. He can start to smooth them out by relaxing more, by not smoking (fact: smokers have far more wrinkles than nonsmokers) and by trying one or more of the following remedies:

Before bedtime, take vegetable oil and massage the lined areas of your neck and face. Start in the center of your neck and, using an upward and outward motion, get the oil into those dry areas. Work your way up to and including your forehead. Let the oil stay on over-night. In the morning, wash with tepid, then cool water. You may want to add a few drops of your favorite herbal essence to the vegetable oil, then pretend it costs $60 a bottle.

It took years to get the folds in your face, it will take time and persistence to unfold.

This is an internal approach to wrinkles. No, it doesn't mean you'll have unlined insides, it means that the nutritional value of brewer's yeast may make a difference in overcoming the signs of time.

Start with 1 tablespoonful a day of brewer's yeast in a pure fruit juice, and gradually work your way up to 2 tablespoonsful—a teaspoonful at a time.

Some people get a gassy feeling from brewer's yeast. We were told that that means the body really needs it, and the feeling will eventually go away when the body requirements for the nutrients are met. Huh? We're not sure what it all means, but we do know that brewer's yeast contains lots of health-giving properties and it may help dewrinkle the face. Seems to us it's worth trying.

The most popular wrinkle eraser folk remedy we found requires 1 teaspoonful of honey and 2 tablespoonsful of heavy whipping cream. Mix them together vigorously. Dip your fingertips in the mixture and, with a gentle massaging action, apply it to the wrinkles, folds, lines, creases, crinkles, whatever. Leave it on for at least half an hour, the longer the better. You'll feel it tighten on your face as it becomes a mask. When you're ready, splash it off with tepid water. By making this a daily ritual, you may become wrinkle-free.

‡ WRINKLES AROUND THE EYES

Mix the white of an egg with enough sweet cream to make it glide on your eye area. Let it stay on for at least half an hour—an hour would be twice as good. Wash it off with tepid water. The vitamins, proteins, enzymes, unsaturated fatty acids—all that great stuff—should nourish the skin cells enough to smooth out the little crinkles around the eyes. Repeat the procedure often—at least 4 times a week.

For those of you who haven't had eye tucks, the nightly application of castor oil on the delicate area around the eyes may prevent the surgery.

‡ WRINKLE PREVENTION
To reduce the tendency to wrinkle, mash a ripe banana and add a few drops of peanut oil. Apply it to your face and neck (remember, upward and outward), and leave it on for at least a half hour. Wash it off with tepid water. If you do this daily, or even every other day, it should make your skin softer and less likely to get lined.

If you eat oatmeal for breakfast, have we got a remedy for you. Leave some of the cooked oatmeal over. Add some vegetable oil—enough to make it spreadable— and massage it into your face and neck. Leave it on for half an hour, then wash it off with tepid water. If you want to be wrinkle-proof, you must repeat the procedure on a regular daily basis.

‡ LIP LINE PREVENTION
The way you may prevent those little crinkly lines around the mouth is by exercising the jaw muscle.

Luckily, the jaw muscle can work the longest of all the body's muscles without getting tired. So, whistle, sing and talk. Tongue twisters are like the aerobics of the mouth, especially ones with the "m," "b" and "p" sounds. Here are a couple to start with:

Pitter-patter, pitter-patter, rather than patter-pitter, patter-pitter.

Mother made neither brother mutter to father.

‡ DARK CIRCLES UNDER THE EYES

If you have access to fresh figs, try cutting one in half and placing them under your eyes. You should, of course, lie down and relax for 15 to 30 minutes. Okay, fig face, time to get up and gently rinse the sticky stuff off with tepid water. Dab on some peanut oil.

When figs are not in season, grate an unwaxed cucumber or a small scrubbed (preferably red) potato. Put the gratings on 2 gauze pads, lie down and put them under your eyes. The rest is the same as above: rinse and dab.

‡ PUFFINESS UNDER THE EYES

We know a man who has so much puffiness under his eyes, it looks like his nose is wearing a saddle.

One of the reasons for puffiness may be an excessive amount of salt in one's diet. Salt causes water retention and water retention causes puffiness. What can be done about it? Stay away from salt. Here are some more suggestions:

When you want to look your best, set your clock an hour earlier than usual. Give yourself that extra time to depuff. Either that, or sleep sitting up so the puffs don't get a chance to form under your eyes.

Okay, you already have puffs. Wet a couple of camomile tea bags with tepid water and put them on your problem areas. *Sit* that way for 15 minutes.

‡ EYELASHES

With a cotton swab, each night apply castor oil to clean lashes. It should help them grow thicker and longer. Another version of this remedy is to mix 3 tablespoonsful of castor oil with 1 tablespoonful of dark rum and swab it on your eyelashes every night. This, too, should give you longer and thicker lashes.

‡ ROUGH, CHAPPED AND/OR DIRTY HANDS

For those chapped hands, try some honey. Wet your hands and shake off the water without actually drying them. Then rub some honey all over your hands. When they're completely honey-coated, let them stay that way for 5 minutes. (We would recommend you read the paper to pass the time, but turning the pages would definitely present problems.) Next, rub your hands as you rinse them under tepid water. In that way, you remove the honey. Then pat your hands dry. Do this daily for a few weeks and, hopefully, you'll want to clap hands for your unchapped hands.

Tired of being called "lobster claw"? Take 1 teaspoonful of granulated sugar in the palm of your hand, add a few drops of castor oil and enough fresh lemon juice to totally moisten the sugar. Vigorously massage your hands together for a few minutes. Rinse in tepid water and pat dry. This hand scrub should leave hands smooth and in the process remove stains.

A couple of simple cleansers consist of: scrubbing your hands with a palmful of dry baking soda, then rinsing with tepid water.

Or, a palmful of oatmeal, moistened with milk. Rub and rinse.

This folk remedy for rough, chapped and soiled hands is a favorite among farmers. Take about ¼ cup of cornmeal, add 1 tablespoonful of water and enough apple cider vinegar to make the mixture the consistency of a loose paste. Rub this mildly abrasive mixture all over your hands for 10 minutes. Rinse with tepid water and pat dry. This treatment not only can remove dirt, it can also soften, soothe and heal the hands.

‡ **CLAMMY HANDS**
Combine ½ gallon of water with ½ cup of alcohol and bathe your hands in the mixture. After a few min-

utes, rinse your hands with cool water and pat dry. This is especially useful for clammy-palmed politicians on the campaign trail.

‡ FINGERNAILS

If you're having problems with breaking, splitting and thin nails, you may need to supplement your diet with a vitamin B-complex and zinc sulfate (follow the directions on the bottle for the dosage), along with garlic—raw or capsules.

The following folk remedies for strengthening fingernails can help if it's in addition to a well-balanced diet.

Daily, soak your fingers for 10 minutes in any one of the oils listed:

- warm olive oil
- warm sesame seed oil
- warm wheat germ oil

As you wipe off the oil, give your nails a mini-massage from top to bottom.

If your nails are very brittle, use a juice extractor to juice parsnip—enough for ½ cup at a time. Drink parsnip juice at least once a day. Be patient for results. Give it a couple of weeks or more.

While tapping your nails on a table can be very annoying to people around you, it is very good for your nails. The more you tap, the faster they will grow. You may need long nails to defend yourself from those annoyed people around you.

‡ NICOTINE NAILS

If your nails are cigarette stained, we'll tell you how to bleach them back to normal if you promise to stop smoking, okay? Now then, rub half a lemon over your nails. Then remove the lemon's pulp and, with the remaining rind, concentrate on one nail at a time, rubbing each one until it looks nice and pink.

NOTE: If you have citrus juice on your skin and you go in the sun, your skin may become permanently mottled. Be sure to wash the lemon juice off before you go outdoors.

‡ ELBOWS AND KNEES

Take the skin from half an avocado and rub the inside of it against the rough areas of your elbows and/or knees. Keep rubbing. Don't wash off the area until you have to go to bed.

Mabel, Mabel, if you're able, rest your elbows in grapefruit halves to get rid of alligator skin. Make yourself as comfortable as possible and keep your elbows in the citrus fruit for at least a half hour.

‡ POTPOURRI OF HELPFUL SKIN HINTS

‡ Instant, Temporary Eye Tuck

You can smooth out the lined area under your eyes. This show biz trick is fine for a photo session but not for anything (date, party, appearance) that lasts longer than 3 hours.

Take an egg white and beat it frothy. Then, with a fine brush, like an eyeliner brush, paint the under-the-eye area. The secret of success here is to paint as thin and as even an egg white layer as possible. As you allow it to dry, you'll notice how the area tightens. Use liquid makeup on top and instead of rubbing it on, gently pat on the makeup.

As soon as you wash off the egg white, lubricate the area with castor oil to help undo the drying effects of the egg.

‡ Face Relaxer

Before applying your evening makeup, take time to get the day's tension out of your face. Here's how: lie down with your feet up. Take a wine bottle cork and put it between your teeth. Don't bite down on it; encircle it with your lips. Stay that way for 10 minutes of easy breathing and lovely thoughts.

After the 10 minutes have flown by, your *face* should be smoother and more receptive to makeup. And *you* should be refreshed and more receptive to anything!

‡ Makeup Remover

Oops! No makeup remover? Use whipped sweet butter instead. (Doesn't this sound like it's right out of a *Cosmopolitan* magazine list of "sleep over" suggestions?)

Whatever makeup remover you use, keep it on your eyes and face for at least 30 seconds so that it has a chance to sink in and make it easier to gently rub off the makeup.

‡ Paint Remover for Skin

A little vegetable oil should clean off your paint-bespeckled face and arms without torturing your skin.

‡ Bandage Remover

When you're wearing a bandage that's not "ouchless," saturate it with vegetable oil so that you can remove it painlessly.

‡ Enrich Your Night Cream

According to cosmetics expert Adrien Arpel, "To transform a skimpy night cream into an enriched vitamin skin treat, add ⅛ teaspoon of liquid vitamin C and the contents of a 100 I.U. vitamin E capsule to 4 ounces of ordinary night cream."

‡ Double-Chin Prevention

If you don't want more chins than a Chinese phone book, start firming up the throat muscles under the chin. Do a simple yoga exercise called "the lion." The entire exercise consists of sticking your tongue out and down as far as it will go. Do it dozens of times throughout the day, in your car, watching TV, doing the dishes, in the bathroom, waiting for an elevator, making a sales presentation(?).

POTPOURRI OF HELPFUL HINTS • 213

It's possible you'll see an improvement in your chin line within a few days.

‡ Nail File Substitute
When you need an emery board and nobody has one, chances are somebody will have a matchbook. File down a jagged-edged fingernail with the rough, striking part of the matchbook.

‡ Polish Primer
Wipe your unpolished fingernails with vinegar to clean and prime the surfaces for nail polish. This treatment will help the polish stay on longer.

‡ Manicure Protection
Use a toothbrush and toothpaste to clean secretarial type stains (carbon, ink, etc.) off your fingertips without damaging your manicure.

‡ Towelling Off
Towels made of 100 percent cotton will dry you faster and more thoroughly than towels made of blended fibers.

‡ Mirror, Mirror, in the Bathroom
After a shower or bath, use a hair dryer to unfog the steamed up mirror.

‡ Pleasing Tweezing
If you can't stand the pain of tweezing your eyebrows, numb the area first by putting an ice cube on for a few seconds.

If you don't need to go so far as to numb the area, but just want to have an easy time of it, tweeze right after a warm shower. The hairs come out more willingly then.

‡ Make Scents

Next time you get sweet-smelling flowers, make perfume with them. Put the petals of your choice in a pottery (not glass) jar. Add some olive oil over them and close the jar tightly. Store it in a dark place for 10 days. Then, strain the perfumed oil into a bottle and it's yours to use.

If you enjoy the perfume and the experience of making it, you may want to experiment with combinations of scents, including aromatic leaves from plants and trees. Orange blossoms, honeysuckles, magnolias, eucalyptus . . . the choice is yours.

‡ Perfume Pick-Me-Up

Dowse a small natural sponge with your favorite perfume and put it in a plastic sandwich bag in your pocketbook. During or after a hard day at the office, moisten the sponge with some cold water and dab it behind your ears, in your elbows, on your wrists and other important pulse points to give you a refreshed feeling.

‡ Sleep

A popular folk remedy for insomnia is counting sheep. We heard about a garment manufacturer who had trouble sleeping. Not only did he count sheep, he sheared them, combed the wool, had it spun into cloth, made into suits, distributed them in town, watched as they didn't sell, had them returned and lost thousands on the deal. That's why he had trouble sleeping in the first place.

We have some other folk remedies to help him and you get a good night's sleep.

In England, it is believed that a good night's sleep will be insured if you lie in bed with your head to the north and your feet to the south.

Nutmeg can act as a sedative. Steep ½ of a crushed nutmeg (not more than that) in hot water for 10 minutes and drink it a half hour before bedtime. If you don't like the taste of it, you can use nutmeg oil externally. Rub it on your forehead.

Try drinking a glass of pure, warmed grapefruit juice. If you need it sweetened, use raw honey.

This Silva Mind Control process seems to zzzzzzz. Where was I? Oh yes, once you're in bed, completely relax. Lightly close your eyes. Now picture a blackboard. Take a piece of imaginary chalk and draw a circle. Within the circle, draw a square and put the number 99 in the square. Erase the number 99. Be careful you don't erase the sides of the square. Replace

99 with 98. Then erase 98 and replace it with 97, then 96, 95, 94, etc. You should fall asleep long before you get Bingo!

This remedy comes from the macrobiotic leader Michio Kushi. When you can't sleep, put a cut raw onion under your pillow. There doesn't seem to be a logical explanation that we could find, it just seems to work.

You know you have insomnia if you can't sleep even when it's time to get up. A relaxing bath may help you fall asleep. Before you take your bath, prepare a cup of sleep-inducing herb tea to drink as soon as you get out of the tub. Use camomile, sage, lady's slipper or fresh ginger tea. Then take a bath using any one or a combination of the following herbs: lavender, lobage, marigold, khus-khus, passionflower, pine needles, lime flowers, rosemary, melissa, meadowsweet (see "Preparation Guide" and "Sources").

By the time you finish your bath and the tea, you should be wound down and ready to doze off.

A gem therapist told us about the power of a diamond. Set in a silver ring, it supposedly prevents insomnia. The therapist also said that wearing a diamond, in any setting, protects the wearer from nightmares. Well, there you have one of the best arguments for getting engaged.

A glass of elderberry juice, at room temperature, is thought of as a sleep inducer. You can get pure elderberry concentrate at health food stores. Just dilute it, drink it and hit the hay.

According to the record (please don't ask us which one), King George III was plagued with insomnia until a physician prescribed a hop pillow. Hops have been known to have a tranquilizing effect on people. Lupulin, an active ingredient in hops, has been used to treat a variety of nervous disorders.

Buy or sew together a little muslin or fine white cotton bag. Fill it with hops and tack it to your pillow. Change the hops once a month.

It is believed by some that the hop pillow will be a more effective sedative if you lightly spray it with alcohol. That's one way of sleeping "tight."

A naturopath we met has had great success in treating severe insomniac patients with goat's milk. He recommends they drink 6 ounces before each meal and 6 ounces before bedtime. Within a week, he has seen patients go from 2 hours sleep a night, to sleeping 8 restful hours of sleep night after night. Some health food stores sell goat's milk. Ask at the store nearest you. If they don't have it, they may be able to suggest a source.

Galen, a great Greek physician, was able to cure his own insomnia by eating lots of lettuce in the evening. Lettuce has lactucarium, a calming agent. The problem with eating lots of lettuce is that it's a diuretic. So, while it may help you fall asleep, you may have to get up in the middle of the night to go to the bathroom.

‡ NIGHTMARE PREVENTION

Lightly sprinkle essence of anise, available at health food stores that carry essences, on your pillow so that you inhale the scent as soon as you lie down. It is said

to give one "happy" dreams, restful sleep and oil-stained pillowcases.

‡ SNORE STOPPER

Lightly tickle the snorer's throat and the snoring should stop. Of course the laughing may keep you up.

‡ SLEEP WALKING

A Russian professor who studied sleep walkers recommended that a piece of wet carpeting be placed right by the sleep walker's bed. In most cases, the sleep walker awoke the second his or her feet stepped on the wet carpet.

‡Smoke Stoppers

Since you're reading this chapter, we're hoping you've made up your mind to quit smoking. Maybe these remedies will help make it easier.

Nobel Laureate professor of chemistry, Dr. Linus Pauling, suggests you eat an orange whenever you have the urge to smoke. The Outspan Organization in Britain conducted experiments with smokers and oranges. The results were impressive. By the end of 3 weeks, the orange-eating cigarette smokers smoked 79 percent fewer cigarettes than they ordinarily would have; 20 percent kicked the habit completely. It seems that citrus-fruit eating, in some way, has a kick that's similar to smoking a cigarette. Incidentally, the Outspan Organization recommends that when you take a piece of orange instead of smoking, first suck the juice out and then eat the pulp.

Marjoram tea can help you be a former cigarette smoker. The tea makes your throat very dry and so smoking will not be nearly as pleasurable. Marjoram is naturally sweet; nothing needs to be added to it. Have a cup of tea when you would ordinarily have your first cigarette of the day. Try ½ cup after that whenever you have an uncontrollable urge to smoke.

According to some Chinese herbalists, magnolia bark tea is effective in curbing the desire to light up. You might want to alternate between magnolia bark and marjoram (above) teas.

‡ CLEARING THE AIR

If cigarette smokers are at your home or office and you don't want to ask them not to smoke, then place little saucers of vinegar around the room in inconspicuous spots. The vinegar will absorb the smell of tobacco smoke. We suggest you also serve cole slaw to camouflage the smell of the vinegar. (Only joking.)

Burning candles add atmosphere to a room and absorb cigarette smoke at the same time.

‡Sore Throats

Most sore throats are caused by a mild viral infection that attacks when your resistance is low.

If you have a sore throat right now, think about your schedule. Chances are, you've been pushing yourself like crazy, running around and keeping later hours than usual.

If you take it easy, get a lot of rest, flush your system by drinking nondairy liquids, and stay away from heavy foods, the remedies we suggest will be much more effective.

NOTE: Chronic or persistent sore throat pain should be checked by your health professional.

‡ SORE THROATS IN GENERAL

Prepare camomile tea. As soon as it cools enough for you to handle, soak a towel, preferably white, in the tea, wring it out and apply it to the throat. As soon as it gets cold, reheat the tea, redip the towel and reapply it. The camomile will help draw out the soreness; the heat will relax some of the tension built up in that area.

According to a gem therapist, yellow amber worn around the neck will protect against sore throats. If you already have a sore throat, it is said that the electric powers of this fossilized, golden resin, will help cure it.

In all good conscience, Joan could not talk about sore throat remedies without including her sure-cure, even though it's in our first folk remedy book.

Add 2 teaspoonsful of apple cider vinegar to 1 glassful of lukewarm water. Gargle a mouthful and spit it out, then swallow a mouthful. Gargle a mouthful, spit it out, then swallow a mouthful. Notice a pattern forming here? Keep going that way until you finish the glass of vinegar water. Repeat the procedure every hour. Joan's experience has been that she hasn't had to do it more than 2 or 3 hours in a row for the sore throat to be history.

‡ STREP THROAT
Do you have a dog or a cat? If you do and you're troubled by frequent bouts of strep throat, have a veterinarian examine the animal for streptococci. Once your pet is free of the bacteria, chances are you will be, too.

‡ LARYNGITIS/HOARSENESS
See the apple cider vinegar remedy in "Sore Throats in General" above. In most cases, the "whisperer" should be talking normally after 7 hours/7 doses of the vinegar water.

If your cold seemed to settle in your throat in the form of hoarseness and congestion, peel and mince an entire bulb of garlic. Cover all the little pieces with raw honey and let it stand for 2 hours. Take a teaspoonful of the honey/garlic mixture every hour. Just swallow it down without chewing the garlic. That way, you won't have the garlic on your breath.

Grate radishes and squeeze them through cheese-cloth to get radish juice. Let a teaspoonful of the juice slide down your throat every half hour.

This is a popular Russian remedy for what they call "singer's sore throat." It promises to restore the singer's voice to normal in a single day.

Take ½ cup of anise seeds and 1 cup of water and boil them slowly for 50 minutes. Strain out the seeds, then stir in ¼ cup of raw honey to the anise seed water and also 1 tablespoonful of cognac. DOSE: 1 tablespoonful every half hour.

Incidentally, just as you don't have to be a singer to have laryngitis, you don't have to be a singer to try this formula.

‡ TONSILITIS

Bake a medium-size banana in its skin for 30 minutes at 350 degrees. Peel and mash the juicy banana, adding 1 tablespoonful of pure olive oil. Spread the mush on a clean white cloth and apply it to the neck. Leave it on for one half hour in the morning and one half hour in the evening.

Juice garlic cloves so that you have 1 tablespoonful of the fresh juice. Add the juice and 2 ounces of dried sage to 1 quart of water in a glass or enamel pot. Cover the pot and bring the mixture to a boil. As soon as it starts to boil, turn off the heat and let it stand until it's lukewarm. Strain the solution.

DOSE: Drink ½ cup of this sage-garlic tea every 2 hours. Prepare another quart of the tea and gargle ½ cup every hour until the condition is better.

The holistic health professionals we talked to believe that tonsils should not be removed unless it's absolutely necessary. They function as armed guards, destroying harmful bacteria that enter through the mouth. Oriental medicine practitioners feel that when tonsils are unable to fulfill this function, it's not that the tonsils should be taken out, it's that the body's immune system needs to be strengthened.

‡ FISH BONE IN THROAT

To help dislodge a fish bone from the throat, swallow the white of a raw egg. If that doesn't work, get professional medical attention immediately.

‡Sprains, Strains, Pains and Muscle Stiffness

For our first folk remedy book, we questioned medical professionals about what to do for a sprain, and we reported the consensus, which we feel should be repeated here:

During the first 12 hours after the injury, starting as soon as possible, apply an ice-cold water compress to the area to reduce the swelling caused by the sprain. Leave the ice pack on for 20 minutes, then take it off for 20 minutes. Extend the 12 hours of cold compresses to 24 hours if it seems necessary. It would be wise to seek medical attention to make sure the sprain is nothing more than a sprain and not a fractured, chipped or dislocated bone.

Since the publication of that book, we've heard about other remedies that have worked wonderfully well. For instance . . .

Immediately dunk the sprained area into a basin of very hot water. Keep the water hot, not scalding, just hot, by adding more hot water during this 10 minute soaking period. Then, transfer the sprained area to a basin of ice cold water and keep it there for 5 minutes. Next, bandage the area with a wet bandage and cover the wet one with a dry bandage.

Warm a cupful of apple cider vinegar, saturate a washcloth with it and apply the cloth to the sprain for 5 minutes every hour.

Take the peel of an orange and apply it to the sprained area—the white spongy side on the skin—and bind it in place with a bandage. It should reduce the swelling of a sprain.

Add 1 tablespoonful of cayenne pepper to 2 cups of apple cider vinegar and bring it to a slow boil in an enamel or glass saucepan. Bottle the liquid and use it on sprains, pains and sore muscles.

Grate ginger and squeeze the grated ginger through cheesecloth, getting as much juice as you can get. Measure the amount of ginger juice and add an equal amount of sesame oil. Mix it thoroughly and massage it on your painful parts.

To relieve pain and reduce swelling of a sprain, crush 2 tablespoonsful of caraway seeds. Put them in an enamel or glass saucepan with ¾ cup of water. Stir over low heat until the mixture thickens. It takes about 20 minutes. Then let it cool and massage the mixture on the sprained area.

This remedy is said to be particularly effective for a charley horse (muscle stiffness). Cut up 3 small lemons,

2 small oranges, and 1 small grapefruit—skin and all—
and put them in a blender. Add 1 teaspoonful of cream
of tartar and blend. Store the mixture in a covered jar
in the refrigerator. Take 2 tablespoonsful of the con-
coction with 2 tablespoonsful of water twice a day—
first thing in the morning and right before bedtime.

Add 1 teaspoonful of catnip to 1 cup of just-boiled
water and steep for 5 minutes. Saturate a washcloth
with the catnip tea and apply it to the sprained area to
reduce swelling. When the washcloth gets to be room
temperature, resaturate the cloth in the heated liquid
and reapply it.

Comfrey is getting more and more popular among
professional athletes and their smart coaches. This herb
helps speed up the healing process and relieve the pain
of pulled tendons and ligaments, strains, sprains, broken bones and tennis elbow.
   Use a comfrey poultice (see "Preparation Guide") on
the sprained area, changing it every 2 to 3 hours. Also,
drink 2 to 4 cups of comfrey a day. Comfrey roots and
leaves and comfrey tea bags are available at health food
stores.

‡ TENNIS ELBOW (See: comfrey remedy above.)

‡ RECURRENT SPRAIN PREVENTION
This applies mostly to athletes and dancers who keep
spraining the same weakened parts of their bodies. Be-

fore a warm-up session, saturate a washcloth with hot water and apply it to your vulnerable area for 10 to 15 minutes. In other words, preheat the trouble spot before you work out.

‡Stings and Bites

In our first folk remedy book (which you're probably tired of hearing about already), we listed the most effective pain and swelling reducers for stings and bites: raw onion or potato, wet soap, wet salt, commercial toothpaste, dampened tobacco, vitamin E, raw honey, diluted ammonia, meat tenderizer, mud, or equal parts of vinegar mixed with lemon juice.

We now add to the above list, a paste made with water and baking soda. It can help draw out the heat of a sting, reduce the redness, inhibit the swelling and take the itch out of a bite. Every half hour alternate the baking soda paste with ice on the stung or bitten area.

Wheat germ oil helps soothe a sting. Every half hour alternate the wheat germ oil with ice on the stung area.

‡ THROAT STINGS

Being stung in the throat is a revolting thought that seems impossible. It's a rare occurrence but it has and can happen especially when eating fresh fruit. Quickly take 2 teaspoonsful of salt in some water and gargle. Keep gargling. The salt water will draw out the poison and, most important, it will stop the area from swelling.

‡ TICKS

This is not a pleasant thought but a remarkable remedy. If a tick has embedded itself in your skin, take clear fingernail polish and drip 2 drops on the insect. It will release its grasp and back out. GET IT! Just wipe it off your skin.

Please don't ask if Shimmering Cinnamon Mist would work instead of clear nail polish. We don't know and we don't want to know!

‡ MOSQUITO AND GNAT BITE PREVENTION

Remember how, when you were a child and got bitten up by mosquitoes, your mother would say, "That's because you're so sweet." There may be something to it. Experiments were conducted with people who completely eliminated white sugar and alcoholic beverages from their diets. They were surrounded by mosquitoes and gnats. Not only were those people *not* bitten, the insects didn't even bother to land on them. Conclusion: if you're sugar-free, it's so long mosquitoes, and gnuts to gnats!

Mosquitoes have been known to stay away from people whose systems have a high amount of vitamin B-1 (thiamine). Before you go to a mosquito-infested area, eat foods that are rich in B-1: sunflower seeds, brewer's yeast, Brazil nuts and fish.

People keep geraniums on porches and other places they like to sit around. Good thinking. The potted geraniums keep mosquitoes away.

If you dread mosquito bites more than you mind smelling from garlic, have we got a remedy for you. Rub garlic over all your exposed body parts before reaching a mosquito-infested area. Mosquitoes will not come near you. They hate garlic. Garlic is to mosquitoes what kryptonite is to Superman.

Biologist Eldon L. Reeves of the University of California tested garlic extract on five species of mosquitoes. The garlic got 'em. Not one mosquito survived.

‡ ANIMAL BITES

If you're bitten by an animal get medical attention immediately!

In addition to professional medical attention, you may wish to try this Oriental remedy for a dog, mouse or rat bite. It requires that you eat aduki beans. Aduki (a.k.a. azuki, adzuki and asuki) beans are available at health food stores. To prepare a portion, put ¼ cup of the beans in a blender. Let the highest speed turn the beans into flour. Next, pour the flour into a bowl, add hot water (about ⅓ cup) while stirring to make it a creamy consistency, and then eat it. Have a portion of aduki beans 5 days in a row to help counteract any toxins that may have entered your system from the animal that bit you.

If you are going on safari, or will be away from professional health care for days at a time, take fresh hot red peppers, an enamel pan, sesame oil and clean white handkerchiefs.

After being bitten by an animal, this remedy has been known to counteract rabies. Use it *only* if professional medical help is not available.

Sauté a few pieces of a hot red pepper with some sesame oil in the pan. When the pepper is wilted, put it on a handkerchief and apply it directly to the bite. When the oily, wilted piece of pepper dries up, replace it with another piece of oily, wilted pepper. Keep repeating this procedure for 3 days, at which time the toxins should be out of your system.

‡ RATTLESNAKE BITE PREVENTION

"Priscilla from Amarilla" (or is it "Priscillo from Amarillo"?) told us that when Texans camp out under the stars, they put their lariat ropes in a circle on the ground, and put their sleeping bags in the middle of it. It seems to be a known fact in the panhandle that rattlesnakes will not crawl across a rope.

My luck, a nearsighted rattler would be passing by and fall in love with the rope.

‡Teeth, Gums and Mouth

‡ TOOTHACHE

Toothache? Until you get to the dentist for the drilling, filling and billing, try one or more of these remedies to ease the pain.

Prepare a cup of camomile tea and saturate a white washcloth in it. Wring it out, then apply it to your cheek or jaw—the outside area of your toothache. As soon as the cloth gets cold, redip it and reapply it. This camomile compress should draw out the pain before it's time to reheat the tea.

Soak your feet in hot water. Dry them thoroughly, then rub them vigorously with bran. No, this didn't get mixed into the wrong category. We were told this is a Cherokee Indian remedy for a toothache.

Whenever the subject of toothaches came up in our home, we would prompt our dad to tell the "pig fat" story. He would begin by telling us that when he was a teenager, he had dental work done and it was on a Thursday. Late that night, there was swelling and pain from the work the dentist did. In those days, dentists were not in their offices on Friday, and the thought of waiting till Monday was out of the question because the pain was so severe. Friday morning, our grandmother went to the nonkosher butcher in the neighborhood and bought a piece of pig fat. She brought it into the house (something she had *never* done before, since she kept a strictly kosher home), heated it up, then put the melted fat on a white handkerchief and on daddy's cheek. Within a few minutes, the swelling went down and the pain vanished. Right about now in the telling of this story, our dad would get up and demonstrate how he danced around the room, celebrating his freedom from pain.

Recently, we've come across another version of that toothache remedy (we promise, no more stories). Take a tiny slice of pig fat and place it between the gum and cheek, directly on the sore area. Keep it there for 15 minutes, or however long it takes for the pain to subside. The dance afterward is optional.

Make a cup of stronger-than-usual sage tea. Hold the hot tea in your mouth for half a minute, then swallow and take another mouthful. Keep doing this until you finish the cup of tea and, hopefully, have no more pain.

Take 50 to 100 mg of niacin to relieve the pain of a toothache. You may get the "niacin flush." Don't worry. The redness and tingling will disappear in a short while, hopefully along with the toothache.

‡ CAVITY PREVENTION
To avoid being "bored" to tears by the dentist, eat a little cube of cheddar, Monterey Jack or Swiss cheese

right after eating cavity-causing foods. It seems that cheese reduces bacterial acid production which causes decay. Peanuts also help prevent tooth decay. They can be eaten at the end of the meal, instead of right after each cavity-causing food. We thank the National Institute of Dental Research for this information.

Tea is rich in fluoride, which resists tooth decay. Some Japanese tea drinkers believe it helps fight plaque. Take tea and see. You may want to try Kukicha tea. It's tasty, relaxing, caffeine-free and available at health food stores or Oriental markets. Incidentally, you can use the same tea bag 3 or 4 times.

Blackstrap molasses contains an ingredient that seems to inhibit tooth decay. Sunflower seeds are also supposed to inhibit tooth decay. Have a tablespoonful of molasses in water and/or a handful of shelled, raw, unsalted sunflower seeds daily.

‡ GUM PROBLEMS (PYORRHEA)
Brush your teeth and massage the gums with goldenseal tea (see "Sources").

In parts of Mexico, pyorrhea is treated by rubbing gums with the rattle from a rattlesnake. (We'd hate to think of how they do root canals.)

‡ ORAL SURGERY PREPARATION
If you eat a portion of fresh pineapple before you have a tooth pulled, or have any kind of oral surgery, the usual postoperative swelling should unswell quickly.

‡ TARTAR REMOVER
Mix equal parts of cream of tartar and salt. Brush your teeth and massage your gums with the mixture, then rinse very thoroughly.

‡ TEETH WHITENER
Burn a piece of toast. Really char it. (For some of us, that's part of our everyday routine.) Pulverize the charred bread, mix it with about ½ teaspoonful of honey and brush your teeth with it. Rinse thoroughly; put on a pair of sunglasses; look in the mirror; and, smile!

‡ DRY MOUTH
When it's time to make that all-important speech, or pop that critical question, you want to seem calm and sound confident. That's hard to do when your mouth is dry. When this happens, do not drink cold beverages. It may help your dry mouth, but it will tighten up your already-tense throat. Also, stay away from drinks with milk or cream. They can create phlegm and more problems talking. Warm tea is your best bet. If there's none

available, gently chew on your tongue. In less than 20 seconds, you'll manufacture all the saliva you'll need to end your dry mouth condition.

‡ CANKER SORES

Canker sores are painful, annoying and can last for weeks. They are believed to be brought on by stress and have been linked to a deficiency of niacin. Take 50 to 100 mg of niacin daily. Don't be alarmed if you get a "flush" from the niacin, although it doesn't usually happen unless you take 125 mg of niacin or more. The redness, tingling and itching do not last long and are completely harmless. Anyway, the daily dose of niacin may speed the healing process and also prevent a recurrence of the sores.

Get an ear of corn, discard the kernels and burn a little piece of cob at a time. Apply the cob ashes to the canker sore 3 to 5 times a day. (Too bad this isn't a remedy for the toes. We'd have "cob on the corn.")

Several times throughout the day, keep a glob of blackstrap molasses in your mouth on the canker sore. Molasses has extraordinary healing properties.

According to psychic healer Edgar Cayce castor oil is soothing and promotes healing of canker sores. Dab the sore with it each time the pain reminds you it's there.

‡ COLD SORES AND FEVER BLISTERS

Speed up the healing process of a cold sore by cutting a clove of garlic in half and rubbing it on the sore. Not pleasant, but effective.

Combine 1 tablespoonful of apple cider vinegar with 3 tablespoonsful of honey (preferably raw honey) and dab the sore with the mixture in the morning, late afternoon and at night.

Grind up a few walnuts and mix them with 1 teaspoonful of cocoa butter. Apply this "nutty-butter" salve to the sore twice a day. The sore should be gone in 3 or 4 days.

Lysine may inhibit the growth of herpes viruses that cause cold sores and fever blisters. Take one L-lysine 500 mg tablet daily with dinner. See "Herpes" for more useful information.

This folk remedy came to us from several folks across the country. If they weren't embarrassed to tell it to us, we won't be to tell it to you. Use earwax (your own, of course) on your cold sore or fever blister.

‡ BAD BREATH (HALITOSIS)
While no one ever dies of bad breath, it sure can kill a relationship. Here are some refreshing remedies that are worth a try:

Suck on a piece of cinnamon bark to sweeten your breath. Cinnamon sticks come in jars or can be bought loose at some food specialty shops. It can also satisfy a craving for a high-calorie treat.

Bad breath is sometimes due to food particles decaying in between one's teeth. If that's the case, use dental floss and brush after every meal.

Take a piece of 100 percent wool—preferably white and not dyed—put ½ teaspoonful of raw honey on the fabric and massage your upper gums with it. Put another ½ teaspoonful of raw honey on it and massage the lower gums with it. Did you say that sounds crazy? We can't argue with you there.

Stock up on mint, rosemary and fennel seeds, so you can prepare an effective mouthwash for yourself. For each daily portion, use ⅓ teaspoonful of each of the 3 dried herbs. Pour 1 cup of just-boiled water over the mint, rosemary and fennel seeds, cover the cup and let it steep for 10 minutes. Then strain it. At that point, it should be cool enough for you to rinse with. You might also want to swallow a little of it. It's wonderful for digestion which may be causing the bad breath to begin with.

At bedtime, take a piece of myrrh the size of a pea, and let it dissolve in your mouth. Since myrrh is an antiseptic and can destroy the germs that may cause the problem, hopefully you can say "Bye-bye dragon breath!"

It is believed that some cases of halitosis are caused by the stomach's faulty production of hydrochloric acid.

It is also believed that niacin can regulate and even cure the problem. Taking niacin is quite an experience. Some people temporarily turn brick red all over from it. Joan gets horrible stomach pains for a few minutes, turns red all over and itches. To prevent the niacin flush, take no more than 50 mg to 100 mg at any one time. Niacinamide offers the same benefits and none of the side effects.

When leaving an Indian restaurant have you ever noticed a bowl filled with seeds that were there for the taking? They are, most likely, anise. Suck on a few of those licorice-tasting seeds to sweeten your breath.

You may want to have a bowl of anise at your next dinner party.

‡ ONION AND GARLIC BREATH

Suck a lemon! It should make your onion or garlic breath disappear. Some people get better results when they add salt to the lemon, then suck it. (That's also a good remedy for getting rid of hiccups.)

‡Ulcers

One of the major causes of an ulcer is the inability to healthfully handle high-pressure jobs, emotional upsets, fatigue, nervous anxiety and chronic tension.

If you're a member of this "fret set," we will give you remedies for the ulcer, but you have to remedy the cause. Change jobs, meditate, look into self-help seminars, or do something appropriate to transform your specific problem into something positive.

And now, we're asking you nicely: Please don't try any of these remedies without your doctor's blessing, okay?

According to a report in *Practical Gastroenterology*, "Aside from its failure to promote healing of gastric ulceration, the bland diet has other shortcomings: It is not palatable, and it is too high in fat and too low in roughage."

We also read that milk may not be the cure-all we all thought it was. It may neutralize stomach acid at first, but because of its calcium content, gastrin is secreted. Gastrin is a hormone that encourages the release of more acid.

A high-fiber diet is believed to be best for treatment of ulcers and prevention of relapses.

If your doctor approves, take 1 tablespoonful of olive oil in the morning and 1 tablespoonful in the evening. It may soothe and heal the mucous membrane that lines the stomach.

Barley and barley water are a soothing food and drink that help rebuild the stomach lining. Boil 2 ounces of pearled barley in 6 cups of water until there's about one half the water—3 cups—left in the pot. Strain. If necessary, add honey and lemon to taste, and drink. Eat the barley in soup, stew or by itself.

Recent research has substantiated the effectiveness of cabbage juice, a century-old folk remedy, for relief of ulcers. While today's pressured lifestyle is quite conducive to ulcers, we, at least, have modern machinery to help with the cure: a juice extractor. Juice a cup of cabbage juice and drink it right before each meal, then another cup before bedtime. Make sure the cabbage is fresh, not wilted. Also, drink the juice as soon as you prepare it. In other words, don't prepare it ahead of time and refrigerate it. It loses a lot of value that way. According to reports on test groups, pain, symptoms and ulcers disappeared within 2 to 3 weeks after starting the cabbage juice regimen.

‡Varicose Veins

You may be able to stop the varicose veins from getting worse simply by the way you sit. *Never* sit with your legs crossed. In a relaxed way, keep your knees and ankles together and slightly slant your legs. It's graceful looking and doesn't add to the congestion that promotes varicose veins.

Folk medicine practitioners throughout Europe have been known to help shrink varicose veins by recommending the application of apple cider vinegar. Once in the morning and once in the evening, soak a cheesecloth bandage in the vinegar and wrap it around the affected area. Lie down, raise your legs and relax that way for at least a half hour. It will benefit more than just your varicose vein condition. After each vinegar wrap session, drink 2 teaspoonsful of the vinegar in a cup of warm water. The practitioners tell us that by the end of one month, the veins shrink enough for there to be a noticeable difference.

In between the vinegar wraps, don't forget to sit properly (see the remedy above).

‡Vertigo

We've talked to hundreds of people across the country about their ailments and not one complained of vertigo. Like skate keys, beehive hairdos and the twist, vertigo seems to be a thing of the past. In all our travels and research, we found only one remedy we'd like to relay, in case there's someone who does suffer the disorienting symptoms of vertigo. Boil crab apples until they're soft and mushy. Every hour, eat a teaspoonful.

‡Weight Control

This "weighty" subject is close to our heart, hips, thighs, midriff, stomach and every other place we can pinch an inch or two or ten.

As hundreds of books and articles tell us, losing weight is hard; keeping it off is harder.

Most people go *on* a diet, living for the moment they can go *off* the diet.

The answer, then, is *not* to go on a diet. If you're not on a diet to begin with, you can't go off it, right?

We found some folk remedies that may help you lose weight without a temporary, I-can't-wait-to-go-off-it diet.

So, put some inspirational signs on your refrigerator—
NOTHING STRETCHES SLACKS LIKE SNACKS!
TO INDULGE IS TO BULGE!
THOSE WHO LOVE RICH FOOD AND COOK IT, LOOK IT!
—and start to practice "girth control."

NOTE: As for diet pills, they can be very helpful. Twice a day, we suggest you spill them on the floor and pick them up one at a time. It's great exercise, especially for the waistline.

‡ BASIC REDUCING PRINCIPLES

Try eating your larger meals early rather than late in the day. This gives your body lots of time to digest and burn off the calories. We've come across an appropriate saying: "Eat like a king in the morning, a prince at noon and a pauper in the evening." While it's not always practical to have a 4-course breakfast, you may want to eat a big lunch and a small dinner whenever you can.

DO NOT DRINK ANY LIQUIDS DURING OR RIGHT AFTER A MEAL! This is one of the most important statements in this chapter and in the entire book.

Water, or any drink, dilutes our digestive juices, preventing them from doing the best job possible. Some sources recommend you wait at least 2 hours after eating before you take a drink of any kind. Our research leads us to believe you should wait 3 to 3½ hours—the time it takes for the stomach to empty after a meal.

Since the body seems to retain liquids one drinks during or right after the intake of food, eliminating those liquids could make a big difference in one's weight. We heard great success stories from people who lost 10 to 15 pounds in 2 weeks, without changing their diets, but just cutting out all beverages during and after meals.

It's easy to control thirst if you stay away from spicy foods, and eat foods with a high water content like steamed vegetables, raw salads and fruit. (In keeping with good food combining, you should not eat fruit until 2 hours after each meal. All this information can drive you to drink. Oops!—better not drink until 3 hours after you've eaten.)

‡ ANCIENT SLIMMING HERBS

Each of the herbs we're going to mention here has several wonderful properties; the one they all have in common is the ability to help the user be a loser . . . a weight loser.

Please know that these herbs do not give you license to start eating as though there's no tomorrow. These herbs are tools that may help decrease the appetite and/or metabolize fat quickly, but they should be used in conjunction with a well-balanced eating plan.

You may want to taste each herb before deciding on the one to stick with for at least one month. The herbs are available in tea bags or loose at most health food stores, or see "Sources."

To prepare the herb, add 1 teaspoonful of the dried, loose herb (or 1 tea bag) to a cup of just-boiled water. Cover it and let it steep for 15 minutes. Strain and enjoy.

Drink 1 cup about a half hour before each meal and 1 cup at bedtime. It may take a month or two before you see results, especially if you hardly change your eating habits at all.

FENNEL SEEDS: The Greek name for fennel is "marathron," from "mariano" which means "to grow thin." Fennel is known to metabolize and throw off fatty substances through the urine. Fennel is rich in vitamin A and is wonderful for the eyes. It also aids digestion.

CLEAVERS: Like fennel seeds, cleavers is not known to lessen one's appetite, but to somehow accelerate fat metabolism. It's also a natural diuretic and can help relieve constipation. You may want to combine cleavers with fennel seeds as your daily drink.

RASPBERRY LEAVES: As well as its reputation as a reducing aid, raspberry leaf tea is said to help control diarrhea and nausea, help eliminate canker sores, and make pregnancy, delivery and postdelivery easier for the mother-to-be.

YERBA MATÉ (Paraguay tea): We've heard that South American medical authorities who have studied yerba maté, have concluded that this popular beverage can improve one's memory, nourish the smooth tissues of the intestines, increase respiratory power, help prevent infection and is a tonic to the brain, nerves and spine, as well as an appetite depressant and a digestive aid.

NOTE: Yerba maté contains caffeine (not as much as coffee). We were told that while it may act as a stimulant, it does not interfere with sleep.

HOREHOUND: This southwestern United States and Mexican herb is a diuretic and used in cases of indigestion, colds, coughs and asthma. It is also reported to be an effective aid for weight reduction.

It most probably took you a while to reach your current weight. And it will take you a while to lose it. Be patient with yourself and give the herbs time to do their stuff. You can help it along by eliminating or at least cutting down on foods with sugar, salt and white flour.

Within a couple of months, you should be ready for the Nobelly Prize!

‡ (NONHERBAL) SLIMMING SUGGESTIONS

We have a friend who's a light eater. As soon as it gets light, she eats. We told her about the grape juice remedy recommended by world famous healer, Edgar Cayce. Since starting this grape juice regimen, our friend's craving for desserts has almost disappeared, her eating patterns are gradually changing for the better, and she's fitting into clothes she hasn't worn in years.

Take 3 ounces of pure grape juice (no sugar, additives or preservatives), mixed with 1 ounce of water, a half hour before each meal and at bedtime. Drink the mixture slowly, taking from 5 to 10 minutes to down each glass of juice.

This Chinese acupressure technique is said to diminish one's appetite. Whenever you're feeling hungry, squeeze your earlobes for 1 minute. If you can stand the pressure, clamp clothespins on your lobes and leave them there for those 60 seconds.

We wonder if women who wear clip-on earrings regularly are slimmer than women without them. Hmmmmm.

A woman we know dieted religiously. That means, she wouldn't eat anything when she was in church. Out of control, desperate and tired of all the fad diets, she came to us, looked in our "overweight" remedy file and decided to follow the apple cider vinegar plan.

First thing in the morning, drink 2 teaspoonsful of apple cider vinegar in a glass of water. Drink the same mixture before lunch and dinner, making it 3 glasses of apple cider vinegar and water a day.

Within 3 months, the woman was no longer out of control or desperate. She felt that her binging days were over and, thanks to the apple cider vinegar, she had the strength and will power to stick to a well-balanced eating plan as the pounds slowly came off.

Lecithin is said to help break up and burn fatty deposits from stubborn bulges. It can also give you a full feeling after eating less than usual. The recommended daily dosage is 1 to 2 tablespoonsful of the lecithin granules.

‡ THE DIET "BLUES"
Color therapist Carlton Wagner claims that blue food is unappetizing. Put a blue light bulb in the refrigerator

and a blue spotlight in your dining area. Wagner points out that restaurants know all about people's responses to the color blue when it comes to food. When serving food on blue plates, customers eat less, saving the restaurants money on their all-you-can-eat "Blue Plate" offers.

‡ LEG SLIMMING
Every night, rest your feet as high on a wall as is comfortable, while you're lying on the floor or in bed. Stay that way for about an hour. At most, your legs will slim down. At least, it will be good for your circulation.

‡Remedies in a Class by Themselves

‡ KISS-KISS

There is a Kiel Osculatory Research Center in West Germany, where they are scientifically studying the act of kissing. One of their findings is that the morning "Goodbye, dear," kiss is the most important one of the day. It helps start the day with a positive attitude that leads to better work performance and an easier time coping with the day's stress. According to the West German researchers, that morning send-off kiss on a daily basis can add up to earning more money and living a longer, healthier life.

Hey, what about us single people? I don't know about you, but I'm going to make a deal with my doorman.

‡ LUNG POWER

This remedy requires an investment of some money and time. Increase your lung power and breath control by taking up a musical instrument—the harmonica (mouth organ). You can buy a "Marine Band" by Hohner. That's a good beginner's harmonica and costs about $13. Hohner also has books that can teach you to play the harmonica while you strengthen your lungs. Who knows—it may start you on a whole new career.

‡ YAWNING

Do not stifle a yawn. Yawning restores the equilibrium of the air pressure between the middle ear and the outside atmosphere, giving you a feeling of relief. And you thought you were just bored.

‡ NAPPING

It is said that a nap during the day can do wonders for balancing emotions and attitudes and, in general, harmonizing one's system without interference from the conscious mind.

Presidents Truman, Kennedy and Johnson were well-known nappers. Add to that prestigious list of productive people who caught some shut-eye on a daily basis, Edison, Churchill and, appropriately *Nap*oleon.

‡ PRACTICE PREVENTIVE MEDICINE: LAUGH!

Author/Professor Norman Cousins used laughter as a medicine to help overcome his doctor-diagnosed "incurable" disease.

According to Cousins, who refers to laughter as "inner jogging," there's scientific proof that it oxygenates the blood, improves respiration, stimulates the body's immune system and triggers reactions that release substances described as "the body's anesthesia and a relaxant that helps human beings to sustain pain."

Looks like your health *is* a laughing matter.

‡ HAVE A GOOD CRY

Emotional tears have a higher protein content than onion-produced tears. A researcher at the St. Paul-Ramsey Medical Center accounts for that difference as nature's way of releasing chemical substances (the protein) created during an emotional or stressful situation. In turn, the release of those chemical substances allows the negative feelings to flow out, letting a sense of well-being return.

According to Dr. Margaret Crepeau of Marquette University, people who suppress tears are more vulnerable to disease. In fact, suppressing any kind of feeling seems to take its toll on one's system. Face your feelings and let 'em out!

‡ CALCIUM CONCERN

The body is robbed of calcium when there is a high consumption of caffeine, colas and other soft drinks. Also, calcium absorption is not as great in people who smoke, take antacids that are high in aluminum, people on a low-sodium diet and/or on a high protein diet. We should all—particularly women—eat foods rich in calcium: sardines, salmon, soybean products including tofu, dark green leafy vegetables, asparagus, blackstrap molasses, sunflower seeds, peanuts, dried beans, corn tortillas and dairy products.

‡ CHASING THE BLUES AWAY

To lighten a heavy heart, drink saffron tea and/or thyme tea, sweetened with honey. (Incidentally, "thyme" was originally called "wild time" because it was thought to be an aphrodisiac.)

If you're mildly depressed and don't want to be, simply change your physiology and your emotions will follow suit. In other words, do the physical things you do when you're happy and you'll get happy. Smile! Laugh! Jump up and down! Sing! Dance! Get dressed up!

If you're not willing to go along with this suggestion, then you're not willing to let go of your depression. There's nothing wrong with staying in a funk as long as you understand that it is your choice.

‡ LONGEVITY

In the ancient Babylonian, Egyptian, Persian and Chinese texts, one folk food is written about in terms of: the secret ambrosia of youth; the formula for glowing health; the magic key to longevity. This folk food is bee pollen.

Take 1 tablespoonful of bee pollen every day and when you're a healthy hundred-year-old who looks seventy, you'll know it works.

‡ GIVE HEALING ORDERS

A Johns Hopkins Hospital survey concluded that 3 out of 4 ailments stemmed from emotional factors. It makes sense. Crises in our lives cause emotional reactions which cause biochemical changes that disrupt the body's harmony, weaken one's immunity and upset hormone production.

We do it to ourselves; we can undo it!

Relax every part of your body (follow the visualization

exercise in the "Nervous Tension, Anxiety and Stress" chapter). Once you're completely relaxed, order your body to heal itself. Actually give your body commands out loud. Be direct, clear and positive. Picture your specific problem. (There's no right or wrong; it's all up to your own imagination.) Once you have a clear picture of your problem, see it healing. Envision pain flying out of your pores; picture the condition breaking up and disintegrating. Say and see whatever seems appropriate for your particular case.

End this daily session by looking in the mirror and repeating a dozen times, "Wellness is mine," AND MEAN IT!

‡Helpful Hints

"NATURAL" INSECT REPELLENTS

‡ Ants steer clear of garlic. Rub a peeled clove of garlic on problem areas and they will be ant-free in no time.

Make pomanders using oranges and cloves (see "Preparation Guide"). Put a pomander in each clothes closet and say bye-bye to moths.

Flies are repelled by thyme tea. Fill a plant mister with a cup of thyme tea and spray around doors and windows to keep flies away.

To keep insects out of bags of grain and flour, add a couple of bay leaves to the containers.

‡ SWEET AND SALTY SUBSTITUTES

When substituting honey for sugar in a recipe, use ½ cup of honey for every cup of sugar. Honey has about 65 calories per teaspoon; sugar has 45 calories per teaspoon. Since honey is twice as sweet as sugar, you only need to use half as much honey as sugar and so you save calories by using honey after all.

If salt is a no-no, use a spritz of lemon juice instead to help provide the kick that salt gives food.

‡ TAKING PILLS

Take pills standing up and keep standing for about 2 minutes afterwards. Taking them with at least ½ cup of water and while standing will give the pills a chance to move swiftly along, instead of staying in your esophagus where they may disintegrate and cause nausea or heartburn.

According to Dr. Stephen Paul of Temple University's School of Pharmacy, a multivitamin and fat-soluble vitamins—A, D and E, should be taken with the largest meal of the day. That is when the greatest amount of fat is available in the stomach to aid the absorption of the vitamins.

The water-soluble vitamins—C and the B-complex—should be taken during a meal or ½ hour before the meal. The vitamins help start the biochemical process that breaks down food, making it available to use for energy and tissue building.

We know people who feel that *powdered* vitamins and minerals are assimilated by the body more easily and more thoroughly. You can buy some vitamins and minerals in powdered form, or you can turn tablets into powder by putting them between a piece of Saran Wrap and hammering them. You can sprinkle the powder on food or mix it in juice.

If you take large doses of vitamin C, take it in small amounts throughout the day. Your body will use more of it that way, and you will help prevent urinary-tract irritation.

NOTE: NEVER take megadoses of any vitamins, minerals or herbs unless you do so under the supervision of a health professional.

‡ DO-IT-YOURSELF ICE PACK AND HOT WATER BOTTLE

Don't throw away empty laundry room plastic containers. Next time you need a hot water bottle, fill one of those containers with hot water. Just be sure the cap is tight-fitting.

You know the plastic bottle with the tight-fitting cap that you used for a hot water bottle in the helpful hint above? Fill it with ice cold water and you have an ice pack.

You can make a flexible ice pack with a towel. Dunk a towel in cold water, wring it out and place it on aluminum foil in the freezer. Before it freezes stiff, take it out of the freezer and mold it around the bruised or injured part of the body.

‡ BATHING MADE EASY

For those of you who can't stand long enough to take a shower, and who find it very hard to get up out of a bathtub once you've gotten into it, make the bathing/showering process easier by placing an aluminum beach chair in the tub. Turn on the shower and sit in the chair. Be sure to have those nonslip stick-ons on the floor of the tub.

‡ RAW GARLIC MADE EASY

The more we read about the benefits of garlic, the more garlic we want to eat. And we found a way to eat it so that we don't walk around with garlic breath. We mince the garlic cloves and drink them down in some water or orange juice. As long as we don't chew the little pieces of garlic, the smell doesn't linger.

A fast and easy way to get the skin to peel off a clove of garlic is to pound the clove with a blunt object—the side of a heavy knife, a rolling pin or the bottom of a jar.

‡ GARLIC AND ONION ODORS OFF HANDS

This helpful hint works like magic. Take a piece of silverware (any metal spoon, knife or fork will do), pretend it's a cake of soap and wash your hands with it under cold water. The garlic or onion smell will vanish in seconds.

Those pungent garlic and onion odors can also be removed by rubbing your hands with a slice of fresh tomato.

‡ GASOLINE ON HANDS

To get the smell of gasoline off your hands, rub them with salt. How did you get gasoline on your hands to begin with?

‡ JAR SMELLS

In order to recycle jars, you may have to remove the odors of their last occupants. For a medium-size jar, use 1 teaspoonful of dry mustard and fill it to the rim with water. Leave it that way for 4 to 6 hours, then rinse with hot water.

‡ WORKING WITH ONIONS, TEARLESSLY . . . ALMOST

In her search for a method of working with onions tearlessly, Joan has worn sunglasses, chewed white bread, let cold water run, cut off the root end of the onion last, and whistled "The Colonel Bogey March."

Recently, Joan heard *Wheel of Fortune* model, Vanna White, thank the TV show's host, Pat Sajak, for this hint: Put a match, unlit, sulfur-side out, between your lips as though it were a cigarette. Keep it there while you peel, grate or cut onions without worrying about your mascara running.

This hint is, by far, the best, but a really strong onion will still bring a tear to Joan's eye.

‡ HOLD ON TO YOUR PANTYHOSE

Onions and potatoes will keep better and longer if you store them in old nylon hose in a cool place. The hose allows the air to get to them.

‡ HERB AND SPICE STORAGE

Store herbs and spices in a cool, dry area. The refrigerator is ideal. When exposed to heat, like from the kitchen stove, the spices and herbs lose their potency and their color fades.

‡Facts, Findings and Food for Thought

‡ "LET FOOD BE YOUR MEDICINE"— HIPPOCRATES

It's unusual to find on-in-years Italians with asthma, tuberculosis or gallbladder trouble, thanks to the garlic and olive oil used in 2 out of their 3 daily meals.

‡ KNUCKLE CRACKING

According to an informal study conducted at UCLA, the gruesome habit of knuckle cracking does not lead to arthritic problems later on . . . just a lot of unpleasantness now: "Will you stop that? You're getting on my nerves. I can't take that cracking anymore!"

‡ THE FULL MOON BOON

Ralph Morris, professor of pharmacology at the University of Illinois Medical Center, did a study which led him to conclude that health problems may act up and can become more severe under the full moon.

‡ A FISHY STORY

Do you have any idea how the custom of serving a slice of lemon with fish first started? It wasn't to cut the fishy taste or to heighten the flavor. A long time ago, lemon was thought of more as a medicine than as a food. If someone swallowed a fish bone, the thinking was that the lemon juice was so strong that it would dissolve the bone.

‡ FEVER: FRIEND OR FOE?

Thomas Sydenham, a seventeenth-century English physician said, "Fever is Nature's engine which she brings into the field to remove her enemy."

It looks like research scientists are agreeing with Dr. Sydenham with regard to fevers below 104 degrees Fahrenheit.

Dr. Matthew J. Kluger at the Michigan Medical School and one of the leading researchers of fever therapy, recommends that fever be allowed to run its course and that it may actually shorten the duration of an illness. Studies at the University of Texas Health Science Center in Dallas showed that fever supports antibiotic therapy. And, researchers at Yale University School of Medicine proved that patients with fever are less contagious than those with the same infection but who have suppressed their fever with medication.

‡ COMING TO YOUR SENSES

The average pair of eyes can distinguish nearly 8 million differences in color.

The average pair of ears can discriminate among more than 300,000 tones.

The average nose can recognize 10,000 different odors.

There are 1,300 nerve endings per square inch in each average fingertip; the only parts of the body more sensitive to touch are the lips, the tongue and the tip of the nose.

That covers four of our five senses. As for the fifth sense, well—everyone knows, there's no accounting for taste!

‡ DOCTOR'S FEE

In ancient China, doctors were paid when they kept their patients well. Believing it was their job to prevent illness, the doctors often paid patients who got sick.

Those were the good old days!

‡ Sources

Most of the ingredients for the remedies in this book are at your local health food store or supermarket.

If you can't get a particular dried herb, seeds, oil, vitamin or mineral, or if you just want to shop around, here's a list of sources that offer mail order catalogs.

‡ HERBS AND MORE

Penn Herb Catalogue
603 North 2nd Street
Philadelphia, Pennsylvania 19123

Send $1.00 for catalog. Money refunded with first purchase.

Nichols Garden Nursery
1190 No. Pacific Highway
Albany, Oregon 97321

If you want to plant your own herbs, fruits and vegetables, request their free catalog.

Nature's Herb Company
281 Ellis Street
San Francisco, California 94102

Request free catalog.

Meadowbrook Herb
Garden
Route 138
Wyoming, Rhode Island 02898

Send $1.00 for catalog.

Indiana Botanic Gardens
P.O. Box 5
Hammond, Indiana 46325

Send 50¢ for catalog.

Herb Products Company
11012 Magnolia Boulevard
N. Hollywood, California
91601

Send 50¢ for catalog.

Herbs of the Three
Americas*
3859 Whittier Boulevard
Los Angeles, California
90023

Send $1.50 for catalog.
Money refunded with first
purchase.

　* Specializes in herbal needs of the Hispanic/
American community.

Atlantis Rising
7909 S.E. Stark
Portland, Oregon 97215

Send $3.00 for catalog.
Money refunded with first
purchase.

Aphrodisia
282 Bleecker Street
New York, New York
10014

Send $1.00 for catalog.

‡ **Canada**
　Wide World of Herbs Ltd.
　11 Saint Catherine Street
　East
　Montreal, Quebec, Canada H2X 1K3

Request free catalog.

Richters*   Send $1.00 for catalog.
Goodwood, Ontario,
Canada L0C 1A0
> * Ships products only within Canada. Complete line of herb seeds and related products for the home gardener.

‡ VITAMINS, MINERALS AND MORE

Freeda Vitamins, Inc.*   Request free catalog.
36 East 41st Street
New York, New York
10017
> * All Freeda Vitamins are 100 percent kosher and vegetarian as well as Feingold-approved for hyperactive children.

Star Pharmaceutical, Inc.*   Request free catalog.
1500 New Horizons
Boulevard
Amityville, New York
11701-1130
> * Special 10 percent discount on first order to people who mention MORE CHICKEN SOUP & OTHER FOLK REMEDIES.

L & H Vitamins   Request free catalog.
37-10 Crescent Street
Long Island City, New
York 11101

The Vitamin Shoppe   Request free catalog.
204 East 86th Street
New York, New York
10028

‡ GARLIC FAN CLUB

"Lovers of the Stinking
Rose"
Founder, Lloyd J. Harris
1621 Fifth Street
Berkeley, California 94710

Request membership in-
formation and applica-
tion.

‡ SEXUAL PARAPHERNALIA

The following company has a sexually explicit, free
catalog available ONLY for adults over 21. When send-
ing a request for a catalog, it is important that you state
you are over 21 and you must sign your name to that
statement.

Adam & Eve
P.O. Box 800
Carrboro, North Carolina 27510

INDEX

Acid burns, 33
Acid indigestion, 129–30
Acne, 186–87
Acorns, 180
Acupressure techniques:
  for appetite suppression, 249;
  for constipation, 45; for coughs,
  47; for diarrhea, 53; for ear-
  aches, 54; for headaches, 112;
  for heart attack victim, 117; for
  leg cramps, 82–83; for tension
  relief, 161; for vision improvement, 67–68
Adrenal glands, 22
Aduki beans, 85, 145, 231
  sprouts, 7, 85
Age spots, 187–88
Alcohol, 208–9, 217
Alcoholic beverages:
  driving after drinking, 107–8;
  easing the urge for, 109; eliminating, 22, 25, 148, 155, 230;
  hangovers, 106–7, 108; preventing intoxication, 108; sobering up, 107–8
Alfalfa seeds:
  sprouting, 5–6, 7; sprouts, 5–6,
  7, 121; tea, 12
Allergies, 42–43
Almond oil, 199
Almonds:
  for enlarged pores, 203; for
  headaches, 110; for kidney and
  bladder disorders, 144; for
  memory, 151; to prevent intoxi-

cation, 108
Allspice, 51, 134
Aloe vera gel, 15, 32
Alternate nostril breathing, 162–
  63
Alum, 100
Amber, 167
*American Journal of Clinical Nutri-
  tion, The*, 120
Amethysts, 108, 152
Ammonia, 229
Amoebic dysentery, 53
Ancient Book of Formulas, An, 8
Angelica, 113
Animal bites, 231
Anise, 48, 58, 217–18
Anise seeds:
  for bad breath, 240; for coughs,
  139; for gas, 134; for indiges-
  tion, 130; for laryngitis, 223
Anisette for coughs, 48
Ankles, weak, 80
Antacids, 254
Ant repellent, 257
Anxiety, 160–65
  see also Stress reduction
Aphrodisiacs, 182–85
Appendix, 133
Appetite stimulant for children,
  137
Apple, 116
  for headaches, 112, 116; for
  sunburned eyes and eyelids,
  35; for vertigo, 244
Apple cider vinegar, *see* Vinegar

somnia, 216; odor on hands, 260; to promote hair growth, 99; storing, 261; for tension reduction, 161; working with, without tears, 261

Onion juice:
  for age spots, 187–88; for diarrhea, 52; for enlarged prostate, 147

Oral surgery preparation, 236

Oranges, 219, 226, 227, 257
  rind for colds, 38–39

Oregano, 131

Organic Consumer Report, 81

Orgasm, 178
  delaying, 177

Outspan Organization, 219

Oysters, 80

PABA (para-aminobenzoic acid), 102–3

Paint remover for skin, 212

Palming, 63, 65, 66, 68

Palpitations, heart, 122

Pancreas, 22

Pantyhose, 261

Papaya:
  for corns, 76; facial, 199; for heartburn, 135; for hemorrhoids, 123

Paraguay tea, *see* Yerba maté

Parsnip juice, 209

Passwater, Dr. Richard, 118

Paul, Dr. Stephen, 258

Pauling, Dr. Linus, 219

Peanut butter, 104, 108

Peanut oil, 121–22, 205, 206

Peanuts, 235

Pepper:
  cayenne, *see* Cayenne pepper; hot red, 231–32

Peppermint tea:
  when breastfeeding, 88; for diarrhea, 52; after gallbladder surgery, 92; for heartburn, 135

Performance anxiety, 174

Perfume, 179, 214

Permanent, removing odor of a, 104

Pernod, 107

Persimmons, 46, 100, 106

Petroleum jelly, 49, 192, 200

Phlebitis, 169

Phosphorus, 175

Pig fat, 233–34

Pills, taking, 257–58

Pimply-faced infants, 142

Pineapple, 236

Pinkeye, 65–66

Plantar warts, 195

Poison ivy, 192

Pollen for mental alertness, 75

Pomanders, 257
  preparation of, 4

Pool treatment, green-hair-from-, 103

Pores, enlarged skin, 202–3

Potassium chloride, 64

Potato, 229
  on burns, 31–32; for dark circles under the eyes, 206; for eye problems, 63, 64; for headaches, 112; for itching, 191; juice for indigestion, 130; storing, 261

Poultice preparation, 3–4

Practical Gastroenterology, 241

Pregnancy, 86–87

Premature ejaculation, 177

Preparation guide, 3–9

Prickly heat, 142, 192

Prostate, 143, 147–49, 175, 176

Pruritis, *see* Itching

Psoriasis, 193

Pumice stone, 79

Pumpkin on burns, 31–32

Pumpkin seeds, 175, 191

Pyorrhea, 235–36

Toes, *see* Feet
Tofu, 192
Tomato, 194, 260
Tomato juice, 104, 109
Tongue, burned, 33
Tonsilitis, 142–43, 223–24
Toothache, 233–34
Tooth decay, 234–35
Toothpaste, 229
Topaz, 40
Touch, sense of, 265
Towels, 213
Trimethylamine, 181
Trudeau, Gary, 126
Turnip:
  for aching feet, 77; for bruises, 189; for coughs, 47
Turnip juice, 29
Turquoise, 184
Tweezing eyebrows, 213–14
2201 Fascinating Facts (Louis), 67
Twitching eye, 64
Tyramine, 17

Ulcers, 241–42
Umeboshi (Japanese pickled plum), 153
U.S. Department of Energy, Anti-Jet Lag Diet, 155
University of California, 231
  at Los Angeles, 263
University of Georgia Hospital, 62
University of Illinois Medical Center, 263
University of Michigan, 116
University of Texas Health Science Center, 121–22, 264
University of Vermont, 20
Urination:
  bladder control, 89–90, 145; bedwetting, 137, 145–46; cystitis, 89
Urine:
  bloody, after jogging, 149; as

freckle remover, 202; for rope burns, 33
Uva ursi, 146

Valerian root, 162
Valium, 162
Vanilla extract, 33
Varicose veins, 77, 82, 243
Veal for sun blindness, 66
Vegetable oil, 203, 205, 212
Vegetarian diet, 15–16
Vertigo, 244
Vinegar, 78, 103, 208, 229
  to absorb tobacco smoke, 220; for aching feet, 77; for asthma, 17, for burns, 32; for cold sores, 238; for coughs, 49; as eyeglass cleaner, 70; for the kidneys, 144–45; for leg cramps, 81; for memory, 150–51; as nail polish primer, 213; for nosebleeds, 168; for skin care, 200; for skin problems, 187–88, 190; for sore throat, 222; for sprains, 225, 226; for sunburn prevention, 34; for "swimmer's ear" prevention, 55–56; for varicose veins, 243; for vomiting, 132–33; for weight reduction, 250
Viral dysentery, 53
Vision improvers, 67–68
Visualization exercise, 73, 164, 255–56
Vitamin A, 175, 181, 258
  as vision improver, 67, 142
Vitamin B-complex, 62, 68, 103, 106–7, 175, 209, 258
Vitamin B_1, 230
Vitamin B_2, 121
  for eye problems, 60, 62, 68
Vitamin B_3, *see* Niacin
Vitamin B_6:
  for leg cramps, 82; for tingling and numbness in toes, 79, 82

‡About the Authors

Joan Wilen and Lydia Wilen are sisters, friends and collaborators, working together since 1981.

Their motto, "write and fight," has seen them through 6 books, a 26-episode television series, several episodes of "Reading Rainbow," a teenage advice column in a monthly magazine, a fashion video for Bloomingdale's, countless feature newspaper and magazine articles and, presently in progress, a CBS "Movie of the Week."